T0328952

Cambridge Elements ☰

Elements in Organization Theory
edited by
Nelson Phillips
Imperial College London
Royston Greenwood
University of Alberta

RE-ENGAGING WITH SUSTAINABILITY IN THE ANTHROPOCENE ERA

An Institutional Approach

Andrew J. Hoffman
University of Michigan

P. Devereaux Jennings
University of Alberta

CAMBRIDGE
UNIVERSITY PRESS

CAMBRIDGE
UNIVERSITY PRESS

University Printing House, Cambridge CB2 8BS, United Kingdom

One Liberty Plaza, 20th Floor, New York, NY 10006, USA

477 Williamstown Road, Port Melbourne, VIC 3207, Australia

314–321, 3rd Floor, Plot 3, Splendor Forum, Jasola District Centre, New Delhi – 110025, India

79 Anson Road, #06–04/06, Singapore 079906

Cambridge University Press is part of the University of Cambridge.

It furthers the University's mission by disseminating knowledge in the pursuit of education, learning, and research at the highest international levels of excellence.

www.cambridge.org
Information on this title: www.cambridge.org/9781108727693
DOI: 10.1017/9781108628068

© Andrew J. Hoffman and P. Devereaux Jennings 2018

First published 2018

A catalogue record for this publication is available from the British Library.

ISBN 978-1-108-72769-3 Paperback
ISSN 2397-947X (online)
ISSN 2514-3859 (print)

Re-engaging with Sustainability in the Anthropocene Era

An Institutional Approach

Elements in Organization Theory

DOI: 10.1017/9781108628068
First published online: August 2018

Andrew J. Hoffman
University of Michigan

P. Devereaux Jennings
University of Alberta

Abstract: *An Institutional Approach for Re-engaging with Sustainability in the Anthropocene Era* applies organization theory to a grand challenge: our entry into the Anthropocene era, a period marked by human impact not only on climate change, but also on chemical waste, habitat destruction, and other forms of ecosystem damage. We focus on institutional theory, modified by political readings of organizations, as one approach that can help us navigate a new course. Besides offering mechanisms, such as institutional entrepreneurship, social movements, and policy shifts, the institutional-political variant developed here helps analysts understand the framing of scientific facts, the counter-mobilization of skeptics, and the creation of archetypes as new social orders.

Keywords: Anthropocene, institutional theory, organization theory, political theory, sustainability

ISBNs: 9781108727693 (PB), 9781108628068 (OC)
ISSNs: 2397-947X (online), 2514-3859 (print)

Contents

1 Introduction: A Grand Challenge and One Organization Theory Response

The starting place for this Element is one of the grand challenges for humanity: climate change (United Nations, 2017). The Royal Society and the US National Academy of Sciences call it "one of the defining issues of our time" (Showstack, 2014). The World Economic Forum has repeatedly placed it in the top ten risks and future worries for the planet (World Economic Forum, 2017). Recently, the British medical consortium, The *Lancet* Commission, pronounced climate change to be "the biggest global threat of the 21st century" (Costello et al., 2009: 1693), and in recent months, the government of China has seen "climate change as a pressing danger, responsible for rising sea levels that threaten coastal cities as well as for aggravating droughts in the north, floods in the south and, as it now turns out, the omnipresent smog" (*Economist*, 2017a).

While the actual phenomenon of climate change has a physical science foundation, an investigation into its underlying causes and solutions lies within the realm of organization theory. "Organizations play a leading role in our modern world. Their presence affects – some would insist that the proper term is *infects* – virtually every sector of contemporary social life" (Scott & Davis, 2015: 1). The actions of organizations, as much as those of the individuals who inhabit them, greatly shape how we will live and adapt in a world that climate change has altered. As the goal of this *Elements in Organization Theory* series makes clear, organizations can, at their best, "be vehicles of social progress and the solution to basic problems such as the provision of food, healthcare, education and other human needs and wants" and, at their worst, "provide the tools to multiply the effects of the darkest of human impulses and result in terrorism, genocide, and labor camps." In short, "organizations matter," and it only makes sense, then, to consider what we know theoretically and empirically about organizations in order to reshape, or redress, this grand challenge. The initial question that guided this Element, then, was, "How might organization theory help us deal with the grand challenge of climate change?" As we will explain, that question will be rescoped to reflect the entirety of the challenge we now face.

1.1 Rescoping the Challenge

According to scientists (Rockström et al., 2009; Steffen et al., 2015), climate change represents just one marker of an even broader challenge, that we are living within what has been labeled "the Anthropocene," a new geophysical epoch in which human activity is having a documentable influence on the fabric of the planet. This is far different from the litany of damage we have inflicted on the environment for centuries. Instead, we are now inadvertently taking control of some aspects of ecosystem operations. In this new age, the effects of the world's 7.5 billion people (to be nearly 10 billion by 2050) can be seen through breakdowns in multiple planetary systems, climate change being just one of them.

Such a monumental shift in our physical reality must, by definition, be accompanied by an equally monumental shift in our social reality, as it is the system failures created by our organizational and institutional structures that are the cause of these breakdowns. From an empirical point of view, the markers of the Anthropocene present humans with the potential to render the environment unfit for life as we now know it. From a conceptual point of view, this issue overshadows all prior scholarly work on the interactions between social and natural systems.

In the Anthropocene, our possible futures are diverse – potentially bright or possibly stark. But where past efforts at addressing environmental protection have focused on "reducing unsustainability," efforts in the Anthropocene must focus on "creating sustainability" (Ehrenfeld, 2009). The former will slow the velocity at which we are approaching a system collapse, but it will not reverse direction. Only the latter will address the challenge in any meaningful way. Therefore, this topic must become a major, if not predominant, focus of future work on environmental issues. Such a shift in focus directs an examination of the causes, effects, and responses of the whole of the phenomenon. So, in this Element, we will address the broader and more pertinent question: "How might organization theory respond to the grand challenge represented by the Anthropocene Era?" To answer this question, we must first examine the nature of this grand challenge in more depth.

1.1.1 The Anthropocene Era

By professional agreement, geophysicists have labeled the current geological epoch the "Holocene," signifying an era of relative stability and warmth within the Quaternary Period compared to the ice ages preceding it. More recently, these scientists have noted the increasing evidence of an overwhelming impact of human activity in geological strata. One branch, working with anthropologists and archeologists, has examined the rise of hominid groups and their lasting impact on the natural environment, for example, as one factor in the extinction of species such as mammoths around 12,000 years ago and many other species today (Kolbert, 2014). Another has focused on increasing deposits of carbon, particulates, plastics, and radioactive isotopes. Still a third has noted the extent to which humans have altered broader systems by which Earth operates, as seen in freshwater balances and temperature levels. These biophysical traces, combined with a foundation in evolutionary theory, have led to a reconceptualization of the role of humans in the planet's history and health (Crutzen & Stoermer, 2000; Kolbert, 2014; Zalasiewicz et al., 2016). To mark that reconceptualization, geophysicists have proposed that we have now entered the "Anthropocene."

Currently, the concept is moving through the process of formal recognition by geophysical societies. In September 2016, the Working Group on the Anthropocene recommended a declaration of the International Geological Congress in favor of formal designation (thirty members voted yes, three voted no, and two abstained). The demarcation of this era, its key characteristics, and its underlying model – and, indeed, whether all of science, not just a subset of geophysicists, will accept it – are being debated (Zalasiewicz et al., 2016). To date, three different versions of the Anthropocene Era have evolved. None is mutually exclusive; all rely on one another and some scientists subscribe to more than one.

The first version is the "Great Acceleration" (Crutzen, 2002; Crutzen & Stoermer, 2000; IPCC, 2017; Monastersky, 2015; Steffen, Crutzen, & McNeil, 2007; Zalasiewicz et al., 2016). As displayed in numerous documents (IPCC, 2017; Steffen et al., 2015; WWF, 2016), there have been geometric increases in indices of declining environmental and human health, such as greenhouse gas (GHG) concentrations, industrialization, urbanization, consumption, and species loss. These mirror the trends in the "hockey stick" graph – the parallel and dramatic increases in GHG concentrations and global mean temperature since the Industrial Revolution (Mann, Bradley, & Hughes 1999). There are also indications of recent declines in human happiness, particularly in developed countries (Cobb, Halstead, & Rowe, 1995; Hamilton, 1999) and increases in within-country and cross-national inequity (Piketty, 2014; Sachs, 2008). These data trends suggest a decline in the social well-being of societies, along with accelerating degradation of the environment.

The second approach, "Planetary Boundaries" (PBs), is built upon nine planetary-level proxies that measure threats to global ecological health. Each proxy represents "thresholds below which humanity can safely operate and beyond which the stability of planetary-scale systems cannot be relied upon" (Gillings & Hagan-Lawson, 2014: 2). Hence, they are seen as boundaries, with thresholds that are periodically adjusted based on evolving scientific knowledge and human response to alleviating environmental damage. Currently, they include (1) rapid climate change, (2) high rates of novel entity introduction, (3)

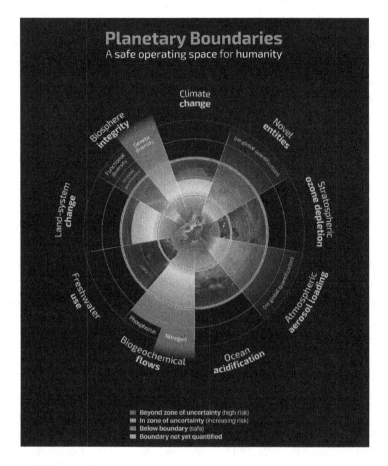

Figure 1 Planetary boundaries of the Anthropocene. (F. Pharand-Deschênes/ Globaïa for Steffen et al. [2015]. Planetary boundaries: Guiding human development on a changing planet, *Science,* 347[6223]: doi.org/10.1126 /science.1259855. Used with permission).

ozone depletion, (4) aerosol loading, (5) ocean acidification, (6) biogeochemical flows (nitrogen and phosphorus), (7) high freshwater use, (8) extensive land-system change, and (9) biosphere disintegration (Gillings & Hagan-Lawson, 2014; Rockström et al., 2009; Steffen et al., 2015; Stockholm Resilience Center, 2016). Each proxy has specific measures for the extent of change (i.e., degree of temperature rises for climate change), and the underlying science indicates nonlinear (often exponential) increases of scale leading to tipping points beyond which return is uncertain. One of the more compelling depictions of this approach, one that has become an artifact for Anthropocene thinking, is displayed in Figure 1. As noted in the figure, scientists believe that we have overshot three key thresholds: climate change, biodiversity loss, and the nitrogen cycle.

The third approach echoes both of the prior approaches but focuses more on consequences or "Ecosystems Breakdowns." These breakdowns come in several forms: the extinction of species (Kolbert, 2014); increased frequency and scale of regional weather events, such as droughts, hurricanes, wildfires, and floods (de Villiers, 2001); and the failures of food chains and water systems that affect human societies (Diamond, 2005). Given the complex relationship among the planet's ecosystems, the breakdowns tend to cascade across different domains, creating ever more vicious cycles and ever greater uncertainty (Rhodes, 2014). Philosophically speaking, these breakdowns are an indication of the limits of human ingenuity and resilience (Perrow, 2007). More concretely, they call into question the economic systems of society that appear to be generating Anthropocene problems (Wright & Nyberg, 2015).

When rescoping the focus of this Element toward the grand challenge of the Anthropocene, we think it useful to subscribe to a combination of all three approaches, as each contributes to the composite whole (Ferraro et al., 2015). In many ways, they represent sequential temporal scales, with the Great Acceleration focusing on the past to the present, PBs concentrating on the present to the near future, and the Ecosystems Breakdowns considering the more distant future should PBs be ignored. All three are based on recognition of linked ecosystem changes, nonlinear shifts in thresholds, peak events, and some subsystem collapses (Ehrenfeld, 2009). Finally, each approach entails specific social problems, which, combined with the environmental problems associated with boundary overshoot, create a composite of the grand socio-environmental challenge that the Anthropocene represents (Biermann et al., 2012; Clark, 2014). So, our reference in this Element to the "Anthropocene" will be the inclusive conceptualization.

1.1.2 Anthropocene Society

As researchers have begun to examine spillovers from the biophysical to the social spheres (and vice versa), they have developed an attendant concept, "Anthropocene Society," to be paired with the Anthropocene Era. Anthropocene Society refers to the human systems (social, economic, political, religious, etc.) that are a past cause, present consequence, and future adaptation of our ecosystem changes (Hoffman & Jennings, 2015; Seidl et al., 2013). Indeed, human systems are the key drivers of climate change, biodiversity loss, waste increases, and declines in human health and happiness for exposed (typically disadvantaged) groups.

There are arguments about how best to characterize Anthropocene Society. A systems approach, which is a natural extension of ecosystem analyses, suggests that Anthropocene Society is best viewed as a complex, multilevel, multinodal set of human systems (Galaz et al., 2012; Polhill et al., 2016; Seidl et al., 2013). This brings to mind a modern Byzantium of overlapping social, economic, and political subsystems that are unwittingly driving and being driven by Anthropocene changes. Within these subsystems, there is a wide array of diverse organizational actors (Hoffman, 2011; Palsson et al., 2013; Schussler, Ruling, & Wittneben, 2014), which include scientific agencies, such as the Intergovernmental Panel on Climate Change (IPCC), the US National Academy of Sciences, and the International Geological Congress; government agencies, such as the United Nations, the International Energy Agency (IEA), the European Union, and the US Environmental Protection Agency; environmental nongovernmental organizations (ENGOs), such as the Stockholm Institute, World Wildlife Fund (WWF), Greenpeace, and the Sierra Club; and multinational corporations (MNCs), such as those in the incumbent fossil fuel industry and automobile sectors as well as those in the emergent renewable energy and advanced mobility sectors. This constellation also includes organizations and mobilized groups, such as climate change skeptics (i.e., the Heartland Institute), the Occupy Movement, the Tea Party, and 350.org. Indeed, the founders and leaders of such organizations often have the same preeminence (and need for accountability) as leaders of scientific agencies, ENGOs, corporations, and governments.

Through these subsystems and constellations of actors, Anthropocene Society and its operation presently lead to accelerating rates of production, consumption, and waste in what has become the globally dominant capitalism-based system. This system has promoted continued growth in population and economic activity as measures of progress without regard for the destructive power that they hold for the global environment that supports human and other life. As a result, various dystopian outcomes are viewed as likely should we continue on our current path. But, concurrently, some hold out hope for a shift in society that will offset some or most of the negative impacts of the Anthropocene. Our goal in this Element is to examine such possible futures. To do that, we turn to organization theory.

1.2 Selecting an Applicable Organization Theory

Because the multifaceted challenges of the Anthropocene take place within systems, logics, beliefs, norms, and the communities that possess them (both large- and small-scale actors), organization theory is well suited for understanding and resolving the Anthropocene challenge. In this Element, we argue and demonstrate that institutional theory is a particularly potent approach based on our broad reading of and experience with organization theory. In particular, we have relied on two converging corpora of knowledge to inform our opinion. The first corpus is research (theoretical and applied) in the literature on organizations and the natural environment, which is found in issue-specific journals such as *Organization & Environment, Business & the Natural Environment*, and *Business & Society* as well as in Handbook summaries such as those published by SAGE (Lyon, Diermeier, & Dowell, 2014), Routledge (Georg & Hoffman, 2013), and Oxford University Press (Bansal & Hoffman, 2012). Relevant research literature can also be found in mainstream journals such as the *Academy of Management Journal, Academy of Management Review, Organization Science*, and *Administrative Science Quarterly*. The second corpus on which we base our choice is found in classics of organizational theory construction, such as Burrell and Morgan (1979), Scott (1995), Clegg (2010), Powell and DiMaggio (2012), Scott and Davis (2015), and Greenwood et al. (2017).

While other organization theory approaches remain useful for examining the question that motivates this Element (i.e., strategic choice, stakeholder theory, and systems theory), we find institutional theory to be particularly applicable, as it pushes in the direction of open systems thinking, which fits with the notion of organizations within ecologies and ecosystems; it incorporates tensions and paradoxes that can allow more fluid interface with natural environment topics; it considers multilayered components of organizations and their environments (such as strategy, structure, technology, and culture); and it readily matches levels of analysis (phenomena) with mechanisms and outcomes.

In addition, recent research within the domain of institutional theory has already begun to examine some key Anthropocene issues, most notably climate change (i.e., Ansari, Wijen, & Gray, 2013; Giddens, 2009; Perrow, 2007; Schussler, Ruling, & Wittneben, 2014) and toxin release (Maguire & Hardy, 2008, 2009), with a focus on topics such as cultural beliefs and values that lie at the heart of a shift to Anthropocene Society. Looking more broadly at the sociology of knowledge, readers will immediately observe that institutional theory is normally listed as one of the key approaches in the literature and underlying knowledge base of organization theory (Scott & Davis, 2015). The institutional perspective, as assessments of article submission topic ("heat") maps have shown, has a significant set of contributors, reflecting a sizeable audience. This should help carry forward institutional approaches to the natural environment in general and the Anthropocene in particular.

Nevertheless, we also recognize limitations within the theory and its ability to fully address certain aspects of the Anthropocene. Critics of institutional theory charge that it is an unchanging and hegemonic paradigm, one that fails to adequately attend to issues of power and dominance (Clegg, 2010; Khan, Munir, & Willmott, 2007; Munir, 2015). As such, we use the unprecedented phenomenon of the Anthropocene to examine and amend institutional theory. In fact, we find that the theory is open to such adjustment and change. Historically, institutional theory has benefited by incorporating elements from alternative perspectives: adding change mechanisms (Dacin et al., 2002), focusing on practice variation and translation (Czarniawska & Sevón, 1996), and theorizing micro mechanisms as part of institutional processes (Lawrence et al., 2002; Maguire & Hardy, 2008).

As a result, our approach in this Element has two components. First, we build on the solid foundations of institutional theory and institutional complexity to construct a model on which to understand Anthropocene Society. Second, we draw on existing critiques of institutional theory as a way to amend and strengthen its approach more generally, and toward the Anthropocene more specifically. Overall, we take seriously the long-term need to combine *Naturewissenshaften* with *Kulturewissenshaften*, a central concern in Weber's work (Weber, 1949), and to use theory and research to inform reflexive practice and policy. Indeed, two of the great challenges for handling the environmental and societal problems created by the Anthropocene are linking the natural and social sciences and using engaged scholarship to bring these literatures most closely in line with shifting biophysical and social realities. We hope to contribute to both challenges by developing a more dynamic version of institutional theory and thus re-engage with these issues.

1.2.1 Foundations of the Mainstream Institutional Model

Institutional theory has only recently been applied to specific topics of the Anthropocene Era, but its application to the general topic of Anthropocene Society is relatively new (see Hoffman & Jennings, 2015; Jennings & Hoffman, 2017). Therefore, we begin this Element by assessing the most current variants of institutional theory and research relevant to the Anthropocene and then consider which parts (or specific variants) either remain applicable or need modification for successful application.

To begin, current institutional theory reflects an underlying skepticism toward atomistic accounts of social processes, relying instead on a conviction that institutional arrangements and social processes matter in the formulation of organizational action (Powell & DiMaggio, 1991). At its core, the literature looks to the source of action as existing exogenously to the actor. But more than merely suggesting that action is a reaction to the pressures of the external environment, institutional theory asks questions about how social choices are shaped by the institutional environment.

Organizational action then becomes a reflection of the perspectives defined by the group of members who comprise the *organizational field*, a "community of organizations that partakes of a common meaning system and whose participants interact more frequently and fatefully with one another than with actors outside the field" (Scott, 1995: 55), generally forming around issues of specific interest and importance to field members (Hoffman, 1999). By interaction, mindset, or widely accepted categorization, members of the field share common ways to understand and act within the world around them. How organizations interact as a field varies. Some variants of institutional theory rely on natural systems views of organizational and field-level operations (collectivist and informal community oriented), whereas others subscribe to more open-system and less-agentic views.

The form of field-level influence is manifested in *institutions*: regulative, normative, and cultural-cognitive systems that provide meaning and descriptions of reality for organizations (Scott, 1995). Of particular interest here, institutions include specific *logics*, which are "the belief systems that furnish guide-lines for practical action" (Rao, Monin, & Durand, 2003: 795); they are sets of beliefs and practices that are deeply held and taken for granted as legitimate explanations of what is and what is not, what can be acted on and what cannot (Friedland & Alford, 1991). One of the most widely accepted expositions of institutionalism, found in Thornton, Ocasio, and Lounsbury (2012), examines how generic logics – such as the market, state, or community – constitute fields and shape actions within them through social orders or systems. Each social order has similar underpinnings in its cultural metaphors, identities, norms, favored strategic moves, and sources of legitimacy and authority.

The social orders themselves are maintained or changed through cross-level, macro–micro interactions. Macro logics, and their associated practices and identity, affect micro-level attention through availability and access heuristics (biases), leading to the use of identity, goals, and schema in communication and negotiation as part of social action. At the same time, these forms of social action percolate upward into macro-level practices and wider identities through decision processes, sense-making, and social mobilization. The strength of this depiction of institutional theory lies within its presentation of the field as well as both its coherent representation of logics (and thus culture) in and across different social orders and its sensitivity to macro- and micro-interactions that shape and shift each logic.

Institutional theory, in short, asks questions about how organizational beha-
viour is mediated and channeled by institutional pressures. As an organization
becomes more profoundly aware of its dependence on this external environment, its very conception of itself changes, with consequences on many levels.
As this happens, Selznick states, "institutionalization has set in" (1957: 7).
Hence, institutionalization represents both a process and an outcome
(DiMaggio, 1988), a duality that helps us examine Anthropocene Society.

1.2.2 The Institutional Complexity Model

Current institutional theory has also embraced the complexity model of institutions (Greenwood et al., 2011; Kraatz & Block, 2008; Pache & Santos, 2010).
This model deepens the examination of how multiple logics work with (or
against) one another within a field and specific organization. As depicted in
Figure 2, from Greenwood et al. (2015), the model relies on notions of complex
fields, which are composed of multiple logics that interact in complementary or
competitive ways (Durand & Paolella, 2013; Pache & Santos, 2010) among
a complex array of actors and their interactions. Organizations respond to this

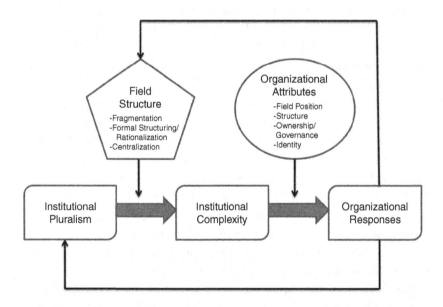

Figure 2 The institutional complexity model. (From Greenwood, R., Jennings,
P. D., & Hinings, R. [2015]. Sustainability and organizational change:
An institutional perspective. In R. Henderson, R. Gulati, and M. Tushman, eds.,
Leading Sustainable Change: An Organizational Perspective. Oxford: Oxford
University Press, p. 327, Figure 13.1. By permission of Oxford University Press.)

institutional complexity with plural logics, shaped by both field structure and organizational attributes. As a result, this model incorporates change mechanisms in a more explicit fashion (Dacin et al., 2002) and explains action as pitched primarily at the mezzo (organizational level), thereby returning institutional theory to its roots (Scott, 1995).

This institutional complexity model has been used to assess environmental sustainability as a problem, but with some modification in its more explicit inclusion of change triggers as jolts, contradictions, and bottom-up performativity, which exogenously affect institutional logics through theorization and reflexivity (Greenwood et al., 2015). To make such modifications with the organizational field more evident, the model considers organizational and individual level responses as a consequence of four proximate factors: (1) organizational positions, (2) organizational structures (that determine whether logics are "represented"), (3) ownership and governance arrangements, and (4) the identity of the specific organization. With these additions, heterogeneity of organizational responses is more likely, opportunity spaces for institutional entrepreneurs are more plentiful, within-firm changes can be understood through processes and mechanisms similar to those found within the field, and skillful hybridizing of practices among firm members is more evident (Greenwood et al., 2015). As we will explain, these considerations will become useful in our amendment of institutional theory in response to critiques.

1.2.3 Critiques of the Current Institutional Theory Model

Current institutional theory, particularly with the addition of complexity, allows for a great deal of research on the natural environment to be combined with and subsumed under its various components. Using institutional studies on the natural environment as one distinct phenomenon for building general institutional models is a valid pursuit. However, it is not able to engage sufficiently with Anthropocene issues as presently configured (Hoffman & Jennings, 2015). For example, it does not directly incorporate the natural environment but views it more as one field or set of issues (see, e.g., Greenwood et al., 2015). Further, the mezzo-level complexity model, like the macro–micro logics model, does not address the possibility that, while institutions and logics are consequential, institutional systems may be fundamentally challenged by action (Fligstein & McAdam, 2011). This is particularly true with regard to micro-dynamics where no direct replacement institution or set of practices is being generated. Rather, completely new institutional patterns are the primary outcome of institutional dynamics (Lawrence, Suddaby, & Leca, 2009). For example, the 1997 Kyoto Protocol on climate change, as a set of institutional practices (Schussler, Ruling, & Wittneben, 2014), was not replaced completely by the 2017 Paris Agreement (UNFCCC, 2017).

A first and strong critique of institutional theory – especially when it comes to handling the natural environment – is offered by critical theorists (e.g., Clegg, 2010; Khan, Munir, & Willmott, 2007; Leca & Naccache, 2006; Munir, 2015; Wright & Nyberg, 2015) who emphasize the central notion of power and control in all facets of social life (Gordon, 1980), particularly in the postmodern world (Harvey, 1990). They argue that institutions themselves are a potent source of systematic discipline and control (Bevir, 1999; Lawrence et al., 2002) but that institutional theory tends to remain agnostic on such issues, asking only questions about who has voice in institutional debates, and no questions about why or whether the makeup of the field is fair or equitable. Critical theorists emphasize that capitalism as the dominant institutional logic of our time creates great societal inequities by relying heavily on power differentials and unequal access to material resources and knowledge.

A second and quieter critique comes from systems theory (Meadows., 2008). Institutional complexity and institutional orders both rely on notions of systems, but neither emphasizes their more dynamic nature to allow for elaboration of the systems models themselves. Systems have nodes (components) and loops (processes), which are linked together to represent the fields being studied (Sterman, 2001). The systems can be thought of as first-order representations, hence able to capture (and simulate) field-level operations; or as second-order representations, capturing the ways in which the main system components operate, such as through system generation, system dynamism, and system learning (Senge & Sterman, 1992). At the second-order level, institutional complexity can be more clearly understood when knowledge about macro-, mezzo-, and micro-systems becomes available (Meadows, 2008). These criticisms from critical theory and systems theory will be instrumental as we amend and apply institutional theory to our understanding of Anthropocene Society.

1.3 Our Element's Design

In the rest of this Element, we offer our assessment of "how might institutional theory respond to the grand challenges created by the Anthropocene Era?" As such, we will offer an "institutional-political" variant of institutional theory for more accurate analysis of Anthropocene Society, both theoretically and empirically. In Section 2, we provide a modification of core elements institutional theory and in Section 3, we present modifications of institutional change mechanisms as they apply to Anthropocene Society. In Section 4, we delve more deeply into resistance from countercultures that deny Anthropocene problems, a powerful component of the social movement dynamics in Anthropocene Society. Section 5 will be devoted to a presentation of three possible archetypes of Anthropocene Society, culminating in Section 6 with a more hopeful possible archetype called Cultural Re-Enlightenment based on notions of sustainability-as-flourishing (Ehrenfeld, 2009). Section 7 will offer some concluding remarks.

2 A Modified Reading of Institutional Elements in Anthropocene Society

In this section, we begin to develop our more dynamic variant of institutional theory, which we refer to as the "institutional-political" approach. This variant is sensitive to ongoing critiques of institutional theory by using the social and economic challenges created by the Anthropocene as a set of targeted opportunities for modifying current institutional theory. In particular, we pay explicit attention to incorporating politics and power (Clegg, 2010; Khan et al., 2007; Leca & Naccache, 2006; Munir, 2015) and drawing on systems theory, which is heavily relied upon to model Anthropocene effects (Polhill et al., 2016). As a result, we offer modifications to three main elements of institutional theory: the organizational field and its communities; logics and culture, and; institutions and actors. For each element, we consider its treatment within the existing literature, offer a modified variant that emerges from a focus on Anthropocene Society and finally, present research opportunities that result. At the end of the section we will summarize our amendments to these three core sets of institutional constructs.

2.1 Organizational Fields and Their Communities

Our institutional-political variant of institutional theory begins with an amended view of the organizational field, building on both mainstream institutional and power theory depictions. In mainstream institutional theory, a field is "a community of organizations that partakes of a common meaning system and whose participants interact more frequently and fatefully with one another than with actors outside the field" (Scott, 1995: 55). Recent mainstream notions of the field have moved away from explicit denotations of field member types and sectors (Meyer & Scott, 1991) and toward more cognitive and meaning-oriented connotations. An implication of this shift is that the joint condition of field members involves more fateful and frequent interaction with three resulting outcomes: forms and practices begin to look more similar and isomorphic (DiMaggio & Powell, 1983); there is greater acceptance of the status quo nature of the constituents and constituent properties of the field (Meyer & Scott, 1991); and there are slower processes of field-level change (Scott, 1995).

But in power theory, organizational fields are social and institutional arenas where actors simultaneously express dispositions, pursue forms of capital, express habitus and exercise power efforts (Bourdieu & Wacquant, 1992). Bourdieu explains it this way:

> I define a field as a network, or a configuration, of objective relations between positions objectively defined, in their existence and in the determinations they impose upon their occupants, agents or institutions, by their present and potential situation (situs) in the structure of the distribution of species of power (or capital) whose possession commands access to the specific profits that are at stake in the field, as well as by their objective relation to other positions (domination, subordination, homology, etc.). (Bourdieu & Waquant, 1992: 97)

Power or capital comes in different forms – cultural, social, and symbolic – and is created through the interplay of structure and agency within the field. Still, much of the thought and action is constrained and taken for granted. In other words, it encompasses *habitus*, reflecting deeper hegemony than is endemic to most fields.

Building on Bourdieu, but also drawing on Benson's (1977) dialectic theory of organizations, Seo and Creed (2002) focus on instability and the inherent change dynamics that are built into fields. *Praxis* becomes a key source of change allowing for "the free and creative reconstruction of social arrangements on the basis of a reasoned analysis of both the limits and the potentials of present social forms" (Scott, 1994: 131). Unlike Bourdieu, these authors depict a field with fewer constraints in field power relations for redefining and shifting consensually generated realties (also see Hoffman, 1999)

Fligstein and McAdam (2011, 2012) have attempted to synthesize these views of organizational fields as a means of discussing mobilization and political action. As part of this synthesizing effort, they acknowledge a host of "meso-level social orders" that have been offered, such as sectors (Meyer & Scott, 1991), organizational fields (DiMaggio & Powell, 1983), games (Scharpf, 1997), fields (Bourdieu & Wacquant, 1992), networks (Powell et al., 2005), or, in the case of the government, policy domains (Laumann & Knoke, 1987).

For our purposes, strategic action fields (SAFs) act as the fundamental units of collective action, where "actors interact with knowledge of one another under a set of common understandings" (Fligstein & McAdam, 2012: 3). Action in such a field is based on who has power and the field's rules for exercising it. In SAFs, as with field conceptions by Bourdieu (1977) and Seo and Creed (2002), there are incumbents and challengers who compete for dominance. Exogenous shocks offer opportunities for these actors to employ social skills ("toolkits") to shift practice and the balance of power until a new "settlement" is found. This dynamic means that even in nascent and emerging fields, disadvantaged groups may gain power by using their skills to overcome incumbents, either individually or by joining with others. The new field's fluidity allows many opportunities for this kind of action, and for the creation of new practice and forms in the process.

Our institutional-political variant treats SAFs as *relational spaces* where multiple and often competing interests engage with other actors, often organized in communities, who may hold divergent ideas about the issues being contested (Wooten & Hoffman, 2017). In keeping with systems theory, such fields are structured by governance arrangements and thus nested both vertically – which implies some hierarchical arrangement of structure and power – and horizontally – which implies some differentiation of structure and power across social domains (Warren, 1967). Within the SAF, there are opportunities for skilled social actors to initiate change but change can also occur in a less agentic fashion. As such, many field-level actors attempt to maintain their settlements and obscure uncertainty in order to sustain the status quo. In the process, the memory, learning, and history of a field become part of the "cultural detritus" (Kroezen, 2014) for skilled actors to employ for either the maintenance or alteration of field structures. In these processes, power is often masked or transformed into the fabric of field interactions and is not as overtly pursued as suggested by some power models. More mature relational fields appear to have an abundance of power dynamics but are bounded and temporarily stable with limited variation in power relations. Less mature relational fields are more clearly politicized, less bounded, and lack attachment to proximate vertical and horizontal structures. In the text that follows, we elaborate on these points and offer examples as we turn our attention to the Anthropocene.

2.1.1 Organizational Fields and Communities in Anthropocene Society

The natural environment in the Anthropocene Era has been characterized by various changes in ecological ecosystems of the planet that depend on key factors, such as habitable land, clean water and air, and bounded climate variations. Across levels, from local to global, these changes have been expressed as key dimensions – as we noted earlier, they are termed the nine planetary boundaries. To aid in our understanding of these dimensions, each has specific indicators for measurement. For example, climate change, biodiversity loss, and ocean acidification are measured by specific indicators, such as average global temperature increases, species extinction rates, and pH levels. Values on these indicators show whether thresholds (boundaries) have been reached or passed, triggering calls for adjustments before and after reaching them, such as the introduction of new and renewable energy sources that reduce GHG emissions and consequent temperature rises. Proper response is part of a learning ecosystems approach, one that has not yet occurred, but for which institutional theory can help us understand.

Some planetary boundaries, such as climate change and loss of biodiversity, entail multilevel (vertically linked) ecosystem measurements that tie directly to activity within organizational fields. These fields have rough bounds with different actors and interests organized around multiple Anthropocene issues. But of particular note, many of these fields are "mature" with multiple defining characteristics. For example, they involve specific scientific measurement, designated actors, and channels of discourse as linkages to the Anthropocene Era; they are marked by field reconfiguring events, such as human-centered agreements (i.e. the Paris Agreement) and environment-centered shocks (i.e. hurricanes or droughts); they are bounded (i.e., horizontal links are avoided); there is an effort to keep fields separate by preventing the logic of ecosystems linkages from prevailing within field-level discourse; there is some recognition of and engagement with disadvantaged groups within any particular field or specific community (i.e. island nations threatened by climate change); and, finally; there exists ready-made resistance (retrenchment) subgroups that may comprise incumbents, such as conservative organizations (i.e., libertarian, religious, and free-market groups), specific market segments (i.e., the fossil-fuel industry) and organized movements (i.e., the Tea Party, Occupy Movement, Arab Spring, and others).

Other Anthropocene boundaries are associated with less well-formed or identifiable fields that might be labeled as "nascent." For example, the debate over the planetary boundary of phosphorus and nitrogen use are not concentrated on or bounded as fields and lodged in specific communities in the same way that the debate over DDT has been (Maguire & Hardy, 2009). Phosphorus and nitrogen are used extensively in the agriculture, mining, and manufacturing industries and discussion of any problems is treated in a more localized fashion than more formalized boundary fields. As such, they are treated separately as toxins and spillovers for remediation or reclamation, using science as a justification for this separate and localized focus. Field-level constituencies that are disadvantaged by these chemical uses tend to be dispersed, located in rural disconnected communities, and are often not well organized, as compared to the farmers, miners, and manufacturers who benefit from their use and are more concentrated. As a result, the disadvantaged groups (including nonhuman biological organisms) have limited recognized voice in the field-level discourse over problem definition and the inequities inherent in solution development.

Both these mature, vertically and horizontally structured fields, and nascent, decentralized fields are joined together and defined by planetary boundaries and systems theory conceptualizations. The imprinting of new fields by older fields through specific institutions and actors may occur, as can be seen in the handling of ocean acidification as a climate change field issue (i.e., with similar scientific bodies and ENGOs). Yet other fields, such as biodiversity or phosphorus usage, have their own internal dynamics and may even disrupt the core field represented by climate change itself. For example, the protection of frogs in biodiversity was linked to climate change for a period but could not be easily adapted to the latter field's discourse; the protection of visible species such as pandas and rhinos followed similar dynamics.

2.1.2 Research Opportunities on Organizational Fields and Communities

We see several research opportunities that emerge from this discussion of fields within Anthropocene Society. The first is the study of nascent versus mature Anthropocene fields, particularly as they form, develop, and move from one stage to the next. Are the methods of organizing and the processes of enacting these Anthropocene fields in society similar, and is this due to classic institutional mechanisms such as mimicry and imprinting or some new set of mechanisms, for example, those around the science of understanding and the politics of the environment?

Second, it is important to delve more deeply into the linkages and disconnections among multiple boundary fields. For example, are the fields related to the planetary boundary of climate change connected in any significant way to those of species extinction or ocean acidification? We can see the connections within the physical sciences, but the interconnections within broader institutional debates that engage field-level constituencies are not well understood. It seems, for instance, that the notion of "global" Anthropocene changes around climate change are being scoped into a series of subconcepts around GHGs, temperature shifts, wind and water pattern changes, and peak events. But only some parts of that discourse and the ascribed mechanisms leak into fields defined around other PBs. The question then becomes, why and in what ways?

A less obvious, but no less useful, research opportunity lies with experimentation around the locus of action for field development. Some fields are best identified and defined at the transnational level, and others at the national or local levels. This multilevel focus has been developed within physical science treatments of the Anthropocene's boundaries, as identified by scientists (i.e., Rockström et al., 2009; Steffen et al., 2015) and ENGOs (i.e., the Stockholm Resilience Center, 2016). But, whether institutional engagement over these boundaries should take place at the local, regional, national, or transnational levels is less clear. In other words, at what level(s) should we normally consider the locus of action?

2.2 Institutional Logics Manifest through Local Culture

Institutional logics provide a coherent rationale for field members' views and behaviors, even if that rationale is not always logical in a technical or philosophical sense. Logics, not surprisingly, tend to arise in fields as expressions of a field's interactions and its deeper structures. They can also be transported into fields from other fields, often through leaders in the focal field in question (Kraatz & Moore, 2002). Through studies of logics and efforts to catalog them, institutionalists have come to postulate the existence of generic logics that form around standard social domains in society, such as the market, state, family, community, religion, corporation, and profession (Friedland & Alford, 1991; Thornton, Ocasio & Lounsbury, 2012). The logics of any domain are in a sense "archetypes" or pure forms and will vary along several dimensions of the social order at particular points in time. For example, there are several varieties of the capitalist market logic that are manifest in different fields at different time periods.

Just as there are many forms of logics that can focus field-level debate, multiple or "plural" logics can also exist in any one field (Kraatz & Block, 2008). These plural logics can be either symmetrical or asymmetrical in terms of their predominance and the degree to which field members subscribe to them for meaning and action (Durand & Paolella, 2013). They can also be complementary or competing, depending on how the specific bases of legitimacy and authority underpinning them align (Pache & Santos, 2010). For example, an inherited basis of authority in family or property law can allow the family, state, and market logics within capitalism to cohere. But in some variants, the state may challenge individual rights by taxing property transfers in families or making ownership horizons more limited in contracts.

Mainstream institutional theory has yet to recognize concern for the natural environment as a generic logic based on social domains, though some have argued it should be (Hoffman & Jennings, 2015; Thévenot, Moody, & Lavaye, 2000; Hulme, 2009). Still, field-specific logics about the natural environment have been researched in the extent to which they are represented in other generic domains, such as the market, state, or community, and within a given time and place (Ansari, Wijen & Gray, 2013). For example, some have studied how global state capitalism among policymakers leads to varieties of environmental agreements (Schofer & Hironaka, 2005). Such logics tend to be weaker (in an asymmetric positions) in most fields (Sharifian et al., 2015).

Those ascribing to theories of logic have more recently embraced culture (Giorgi, Lockwood & Glynn, 2015; Dowd, Glynn, & Lounsbury, 2017) as the "processes of meaning-making ... [that] operate in different sorts of social locations (in more specialized arenas or more generally) and may be evident in all sorts of social practices and social products. The central concerns of those who study culture are to understand processes of meaning-making, to account for different meanings, and to examine their effects in social life" (Spillman, 2002: 4). The characteristics of culture depend greatly on the specific groups and their particular contexts, such as history, social dynamics, and ongoing issues. The more coherent and congruent the pattern of characteristics and the more closely they are tied to context, the stronger the culture. But, cultures can exist in more fragmented forms with ambiguously related sets of ideas and practices, as long as the actors are indirectly guided by them and analysts can discern this (Martin, 2001).

So, cultures reflect the instantiation of logics in a particular group in a particular place and time such that they are associated with particular types of communities (Marquis, Glynn, & Davis, 2007). The logic of market capitalism, for example, while often tied to common practices, such as stock market exchanges (Weber, Davis & Lounsbury, 2009), is manifest differently in Denmark, New York, and Tokyo. As a result, institutionalists studying culture are interested in both the generic capitalist market logics in each place and how these logics differ and shape thought and action. For instance, cultural studies of specific state responses to environmental issues, such as water shortage research, differ within multiple contexts (Espeland, 1998).

Our institutional-political variant of institutional theory views logics through the lens of agency, interest, authority, power dynamics, and hegemony – elements that each logic embodies for expression in field-level interactions. For instance, the logics of capitalist markets use the metaphor of competitive and fair market transactions, relying on share value (property) as a source of legitimacy and shareholder involvement (capital owners) as a source of authority (Thornton, Ocasio, & Lounsbury, 2012: 56). Transactions in such logics require that the ideology of capitalism be strongly believed by all parties engaged (Harvey, 1990). This includes both an objectivist approach to control among categories of principals and agents as well as a systematic approach to the means for assessing action that leads to domination (Lawrence et al., 2002). Transgressions against the logic of this system are handled by recategorizing individuals so that they lose privilege or access and are thus put under professional surveillance and review (Morris & Patton, 1979). Should she or he not evince belief in capitalism (i.e., through party affiliations, market specific behavior, or social movement action), the person is likely to be more heavily sanctioned (Gramsci, 1995).

In our institutional-political variant, culture becomes even more important as a venue for the expression of logics than in standard institutional theory because cultures show all the variable manifestations of power (i.e., covert/overt, passive/active, mental/physical, and impersonal/personal). Culture allows for the plural logics of a field to thrive, while also guaranteeing sufficient domination of the disadvantaged. This is sometimes a difficult social balancing act. For example, the Savings and Loan Crisis of the 1980s and 1990s threatened capitalism in America and the dominance of advantaged groups such as bankers and investors. The disadvantaged in various communities allied with the state to challenge mortgage lenders and analysts. Some categories (i.e., derivative lenders), some individual banks (i.e., Lehman Brothers), and some individuals (i.e., Charles Keating) had to be punished ("sacrificed") before the market's legitimacy could be reestablished. The new turbulent, threatened culture of capitalism received a great deal of retheorizing, both in its ranks (i.e., Piketty, 2014; Sachs, 2008) and from academic analysts (i.e., Lounsbury & Hirsch, 2010). As a result, it is now considered a more contested field and less palatable cultural motif.

2.2.1 Logics and Local Cultures in Anthropocene Society

Anthropocene Society will reflect the generic logics through which the Anthropocene Era is conceptualized and understood. These logics will form the institutional foundation by which any emergent social order may be theorized. As a start, understanding how our current society is moving from impacting the natural environment to taking some control of natural systems can be traced within each logic, such as a dimension akin to authority (Thornton, Ocasio, & Lounsbury, 2012) and through an examination of cultures in particular contexts. For instance, some might argue that within market logics, the focus of Anthropocene Society should be anchored on absolute levels of consumption of raw materials and production of waste products (i.e., carbon dioxide), either in the aggregate or on a per capita basis, as these are key drivers of pollution, habitat loss, and climate change (Wright & Nyberg, 2015).

Alternatively, these logics may be curtailed by community and state logics that anchor on alternative considerations for fairness and equity as a means for redressing our environmental impact (Sharifian et al., 2015).

But, such existing logics may be insufficient to the scale of the challenge that the Anthropocene Era represents (Ehrenfeld, 2009; Ehrenfeld & Hoffman, 2013; Hulme, 2009). As a result, Anthropocene Society may move beyond specific generic logics to the development of new types of logics focused on the social perception of, beliefs in, concern for, and interactions with the natural environment (Thévenot, Moody, & Lavaye, 2000). If concern for the unprecedented human influences on the natural environment is taken seriously as an emergent logic, then its various dimensions in a social order require theorizing (Thornton, Ocasio, & Lounsbury, 2012).

The likely metaphor for this emergent logic is a set of ecological and social systems at higher and lower interrelated levels of analysis, from the subatomic to the cosmological. The bounds of such systems are expanded as they refer to the nonhuman portion of the world around us; what is collectively called "nature." In Anthropocene Society, the primary source of legitimacy for observing and understanding the natural environment is presently through the application of science, though other naturalist methods also have some legitimacy. The authority of scientific truth is verified by the scientific method and applied by the relevant scientific professionals. Indeed, dealing with problems in the natural world by developing policy that is informed through scientific methods is the main strategy of this social order.

The development of a natural environment logic has its own conundrums. In that logic, those who do not hold to the core metaphor of interlocked, multilevel ecosystems may be considered to be myopic, and those who do not subscribe to the facts and methods from science or use them improperly may be considered less legitimate in field-level discourse. But, a proficiency in science requires training and the accumulation of knowledge, which requires time and resources that are not available to all. So those without these advantages will have less direct voice in formal problem solving and policy formation in Anthropocene Society. Another conundrum is that the natural environment itself is typically an asymmetrically positioned, secondary and weaker logic in an organizational field with plural logics. In the case of the medical professions, for example, scientists are highly respected, but less so than medical doctors, and more so than ecologists. The pursuit of human health and its importance to the community, family, and market have thus encouraged involvement of the state to maintain the status of medical professionals. It has become difficult, even with the science of climate change, to find a similar coalescence to bolster the profession of climate scientists in the natural environment logic. Indeed, because of the weak position of the logic, it is hard to find a relatively pure empirical example of the logic within an existing field. Both conundrums will be discussed further in Section 4, under the topic of resistance.

Moving from logics to culture, a culture that is focused around the natural environment would embody the values, beliefs, and practices of field members in a specific field and context (time period and place). For example, the group of geophysicists now proposing formal recognition for the Anthropocene are a community that has its own belief system which it seeks to establish. This belief system privileges scientific reasoning and large data models for explaining reality. Indeed, while each dimension of the planetary boundary model has gained some level of consensus and some accepted measurements (for instance, the extent of climate change is measured by the degrees of warming above preindustrial baselines), the overall model faces alternatives framings. Those who refuse to accept climate science are quick to point out that the climate is always changing and accuse science on the topic as having become corrupted (Hoffman, 2015). Even within the community that may accept the scientific ideology, there are cultural splits. The Great Acceleration and Ecosystems Breakdowns versions of the Anthropocene have strong proponents, but there are also those who subscribe to slightly older models of sustainability, such as the purity of land, air, and water (see Greenwood, Jennings, & Hinings, 2015 or Young & Dhanda, 2012 for a review). So, from the point of view of culture, the instantiation of a natural environment logic around the notion of the Anthropocene looks like a highly contested project: the field is divergent and differentiated, rather than being marked by collaboration and having a core coalition of trained intellectual activists.

Similarly, local or regional cultures exist with strong concerns for the natural environment. Some of these cultures are found in specific communities of organizations, like institutionalized ENGOs (i.e., WWF, Greenpeace, and the Sierra Club), local groups (i.e., communitarian churches, farmers' markets, and food cooperatives), specific religious traditions (i.e., Catholic, Protestant, Evangelical, Jewish, Buddhist, Muslim, or Quaker) and specific political affiliations (i.e., Republican, Democrat, Independent, or Green). Perhaps more than among the actors dealing with the definition of the Anthropocene and promoting its science, these issue- or place-focused communities have less embattled cultures. The result, however, may be that these strong local communities increase the differences across them within the field.

2.2.2 Research Opportunities on Logics and Cultures

Our institutional-political variant's treatment of logics and culture in Anthropocene Society reveals several research opportunities. First, there is ample room for an elaboration of how the natural environment affects multiple existing logics, such as the market, family, community, and state. Second, and as an extension of the first, we need further theorization of the logic of concern for the natural environment, both as it stands on its own and as it connects with other logics through general considerations of key shared constructs such as professions and through specific considerations like the Anthropocene's planetary boundaries and their deterioration. Third, we need to demonstrate how Anthropocene science can and does inform society, and where it is falling short. This domain of study has tremendous opportunities for linking social and environmental analysis, an objective that has been sought but never fully realized for decades. Fourth, the multiple and conflicting field-level constituencies who are engaged by the Anthropocene need to become objects of analysis, including those that are proponents, opponents, and disengaged (Leiserowitz et al., 2014). In each case, there is an open stream of research to examine their role within field-level debates, their culture, and the social skills available to them. Fifth and finally, Anthropocene Society creates an opportunity to bring the disadvantaged within the environment logic more fully into institutional analysis. This is a particularly intriguing direction for investigation, one that can help to more fully develop institutional analyses that have tended to focus strictly on those with voice and less on those that either lack voice or may have latent forms of engagement that go beyond the more visible manifestations that can be measured directly (Schifeling & Hoffman, 2017).

2.3 Institutions and Varieties of Institutional Actors

Institutions are patterns of both belief and practice that guide organizational action and can take on general forms such as regulation, industry norms, or taken for granted beliefs as well as recognized material referents – literally brick-and-mortar organizations. Well-known and often-referenced examples include the YMCA (Zald & Denton, 1963), General Motors (Chandler, 1962), and the TVA (Selznick, 1949). In older institutionalism, material institutions were a powerful focus; today, in newer institutionalism, less material forms of institutions are examined, such as the symbolic nature and meaning of diversity programs, citizenship, and markets (Greenwood et al., 2008; Hirsch & Lounsbury, 1997). These institutions, material or symbolic, based on structure, practice, or cognition, are embedded and supported within fields; the field itself, however, is not an institution but rather the domain of that institution, with its constituent and organizational practices.

Institutional actors are the socially constructed entities engaged with the institutions in a field. The actors can be individuals, groups, or even the institution itself (Scott, 1995), as long as those within the field or those studying the field deem the actor to have some degree of agency (DiMaggio, 1988). For instance, "citizens" are a standard category in modern states and includes most of these states' internal members. But that is a recent construction, along with the rights of those citizens (Meyer & Scott, 1991). The agency of these actors may be concentrated or distributed, allowing them to act in a coherent fashion as an entity or indirectly through other institutional components in a field (Garud & Karnøe, 2003).

In our institutional-political reading of institutional theory, institutions ensconce power in their structures and behavioral dynamics (Clegg, 2010; Giddens, 1984), typically arranged vertically based on position within an institution, where that power reflects the legitimated artifacts of the specific logic or in situ culture. For example, an evident authority system in an institution sets the rules and goals that exert control on institutional members. The pervasiveness of the institution and its deep legitimacy leads this power to appear objective, like some form of faceless domination (Foucault, 1977). The state and other supra-institutions (such as stock markets or churches) have particular importance as power-based entities. They act as legitimators and maintainers of institutions and are able to identify and label individuals and their behavior as "exemplary," and hence worthy of reward, or "deviant," and thus worthy of sanctions.

However, we do not see fields as neatly organized and monolithic domains, as some readings would suggest. Institutions compete with others for power. Some are more flat and decentralized, while others are more hierarchical. For example, the state is composed of many agencies and leaders, and only periodically acts as a unified actor on issues (Allison, 1971; Laumann & Knoke, 1987). Further, actors in institutions are divided into those with more and those with less power: the elites and the dominated. Elites tend to defend access and privilege in institutions and act as a source of retrenchment (Foucault, 1977). In knowledge-based institutions and fields, skeptics or contrarians are often among the elites and can delegitimate change. Nonelites are the dominated and objectified targets of power and control. They are often specific individuals or classes of individuals that seek to move from nonelite to elite status by amassing cultural currency (Bourdieu, 2011). But entrenched elites may seek to impose discipline to keep them in their demoted status. Both the dominated and elites can mobilize action and seek to enhance their power, even if it is modest. We will discuss their mobilization of nonelites under the topic of institutional change in Section 3.

2.3.1 Institutions and Institutional Actors in Anthropocene Society

The Anthropocene, as observed and understood using systems thinking, can be seen as a form of complex systems, with feedback loops for processes and nodes for key decision points (Polhill et al., 2016; Seidl et al., 2013). Many of these loops are standardized interactions of the ecosystem, such as seasonal rainfall leading to springtime growth. These loops can be virtuous or vicious, reinforcing or destabilizing. The reinforced and more virtuous (fecund) loops are considered the goal and hallmark of most naturally selected ecosystems (Marshall & Brown, 2003). But in the Anthropocene, destabilized, vicious loops and subsystem collapses are more likely. In some cases, these eroding, periodically collapsing systems have been framed as the new normal, and therefore institutionalized.

Actors in these ecosystems are all sentient organisms involved in different subsystems. It is not uncommon to hear animals of various sorts, not just humans, discussed as either members or actors. The more active or agentic actors are those at key nodes (i.e., decision points, choices areas, and system shifts) in the ecosystems while less agentic actors occupy less powerful peripheral nodes or places with great deals of redundancy. Given that human systems are increasingly central parts of these ecosystems in the Anthropocene, human actors have increasing importance within them. Scientist and technicians are very central and critical, and hence powerful actors. Regulators and those who form policy also occupy powerful nodes in the system. Corporations, while viewed as members of the systems, are often viewed as self-interested and nonconstructive actors that help create ecosystem decline and periodic system collapses, though some corporate activities that address environmental problems challenge that depiction (Hoffman, 2018).

Drawing on some of this system thinking for our institutional-political view of Anthropocene Society, we argue that institutions engaged centrally and critically with the natural environment are becoming far more important than they have been in prior institutional analyses. Given the grand scale of the Anthropocene challenges, these would-be global or "transnational" institutions have either a substantial negative or positive impact on the environment. In other words, they create, make decisions about, or offer solutions to the environmental problems we face. Many such institutions bridge from science to policy, and frequently from communities to the state. They are generally very large national – private or public – organizations that have meaning and interact centrally in fields. Examples include the United Nations, Greenpeace, and other organization that have enduring symbolic and substantive importance.

But, as a less obvious point, these institutions would also include other, less traditionally prominent organizations that are brought to the fore because of Anthropocene issues. Examples are the Chinese and Indian NGOs and ENGOs (either arms of international organizations or stand-alone national entities) that seek to inject new interests into global discourse. Two specific and highly successful instances are China's Pandas International and India's Project Tiger. The less evident groups of institutions also include organizations that work on specific dimensions or clusters of Anthropocene boundaries. The Association of Zoos and Aquariums coordinates breeding programs for endangered species, often facing challenges resulting from habitat changes as a result of toxins, urbanization, or shifts in food chains. Farmers' markets and Local Food and Slow Food are also Anthropocene organizations of interest, for they seek to gain recognition for the use of organic production methods, local sources, and traditional means of preparation to circumvent many of the toxins and destructive habitat practices of other forms of industrial farming and food preparation.

Still, many of these institutions, actors, and practices are populated more by elites lodged in affluent locales. As we move to more disadvantaged contexts or more peripheral areas of fields, this is an important consideration for our political variant of institutional theory. We see organizational actors that do not yet have the wider acceptance, power, or voice within institutional discourse (by traditional measures) as potential "institutions" that are in "proto-institutional" states (Lawrence et al., 2002). To leave them out of institutional analysis creates an incomplete assessment of fields and institutions, as their presence can affect institutional processes and outcomes, whether suddenly, indirectly, or through proxies (Schifeling & Hoffman, 2017). Such actors might include regional organizations representing nations impacted by climate change damage, such as the OASIS Hub and ASEAN (Association of Southeast Asian Nations), which are concerned with human displacements due to sea level rise, and funds such as Global Giving, which has been donating to the Caribbean and Puerto Rico hurricane relief effort. They might also include on-the-ground efforts, such as Black Mamba, the female antipoaching unit in South Africa, or OWL (Orphaned Wildlife), a nonprofit organization in the northwest of North America dedicated to saving raptors.

2.3.2 Research Opportunities on Institutions and Institutional Actors

The research opportunities for studying institutions and actors are in keeping with the call from Davis and Marquis (2005) to study phenomena. We see a need to catalog, sort, and study institutions and organizations associated with the various dimensions of the Anthropocene in the same way that green organizations have been analyzed elsewhere (i.e., see Hoffman & Bertels, 2010). While we would suggest starting with ENGOS, we also think that focusing on organizations that are developing solutions (i.e., clean technologies, organic foods, or alternative mobility) is equally important. Additionally, we also need systematic effort at identifying and cataloguing lower-profile organizations in disadvantaged contexts that are impacting local discourse or influencing global discourse indirectly, either now or potentially in the future. Given the dispersed and disparate nature of these organizations, methodological approaches will be necessary that go beyond standard information sources that typically favor powerful and centrally located actors (see Appendix). Finally, more research and cataloguing of skeptic or oppositional groups must be gathered to round out a complete assessment of the entire field that is forming around Anthropocene Society (see the topic of resistance in Section 4). Based on the corpus of this basic information around membership, operation, and specific subgroups of field members and institutions, we might be able to develop a more unique and informed set of statements about institutions in Anthropocene Society.

2.4 Conclusion

In this section, we have modified institutional theory by considering both critical theory challenges and the need to engage with systems models used in natural sciences before applying institutional theory to the grand challenge of the Anthropocene. These amendments to the key elements of mainstream institutional theory are summarized in Table 1. We hope these amendments will provide a more theoretically congruent and applicable set of constructs for handling different Anthropocene issues. In the next section, we will turn to the change mechanisms in institutional theory.

3 A Modified Reading of Institutional Change Mechanisms in Anthropocene Society

Institutional change mechanisms are evident in the mainstream institutional model discussed in Sections 1 and 2. Both the logic model of Thornton, Ocasio and Lounsbury (2012) and the institutional complexity model of Greenwood et al. (2011) offer loops with key mechanisms for institutionalization and actor response. In these models, there are change triggers and field-level theorization about problems and solutions, with attention and sense-making as important components (also see Greenwood et al., 2008; Lawrence, Suddaby, & Leca,

Table 1. Amendments to Institutional Theory Elements in Light of the Anthropocene

Theoretical Elements	Institutional-Political Variant	Application to Anthropocene Society
Organizational fields and their communities	A relational space where multiple and often competing actors and interests engage with other actors who may hold divergent ideas about the issue(s) being contested. Various communities of these actors exist in fields and create the constellation of interests observed. Fields tend toward instability and flux, depending on the dynamics of their specific communities	Relational spaces are organized around key contested Anthropocene issues, many as extensions of boundary conditions (e.g., climate change, species extinction, habitat destruction). Communities of varying coherence exist around these issues. The linkages across fields and the nature of science, technology, and education professionals tend to create vertically and horizontally complex, partly stable fields.
Institutional logics manifest in local cultures	Fields have multiple logics, but they are usually asymmetric and reinforce a dominant logic. Interest, agency, types of control, and methods of contestation are defined by the dominant logic(s); methods of engagement are typically rational and justified. The logic is manifest if local cultures in the field. In mature fields, there is usually a mainstream culture in a dominant community.	Anthropocene Society incorporates ecosystems into logics of operation, science and technology. But it remains a secondary, Anthropocene logic that is not well theorized and more accurately depicted as a set of "institutional archetypes" that are mixed together in specific cultures of a field's communities.

| Institutions and institutional actors | Institutions are enduring, taken for granted sets of beliefs and practices that inherently reflect interest and agency. As a result, they are normally the focus of action and a source of power for some key actors. Elites, in particular, try to maintain power in fields by utilizing institutions to maintain and project their interests. | Institutions are taken for granted and affect, positively or negatively, Anthropocene thresholds. There are new environmentally oriented institutions and actors of note in both advantaged and disadvantaged contexts. These institutions often threaten the economic, political, and power interests of incumbent elites. |

2009). These models also contain key decision makers or groups of mobilized actors that select, sort, or build new solutions that are gradually diffused and accepted within the field.

In other words, since the early 2000s, triggers or shocks (Dacin et al., 2002; Hoffman & Ocasio, 2001), leaders (Kraatz & Moore, 2002), mobilized actors (Davis et al., 2005), and creative agents (Maguire & Hardy, 2009) have become accepted as key components for institutional change. However, each of these components has also been examined within political approaches to organizations. So, consistent with our intention to develop an institutional-political variant of institutional theory that locates power and politics more centrally, we will briefly review these mechanisms, and then amend them in order to offer a stronger model for assessing change in Anthropocene Society. Our examination will focus on three primary change mechanisms: triggers, disruptive events, and cultural anomalies; institutional entrepreneurs and social mobilization; and regulatory change agents and policy.

3.1 Triggers, Disruptive Events, and Cultural Anomalies

In traditional institutional theory, new ideas and practices that enter and diffuse through a field are triggers for institutionalization (Tolbert & Zucker, 1983). These triggers are considered exogenous and might lead to new substantive or symbolic practices, based on their nature. Triggers that are at odds with incumbent organizational or institutional practice are likely to be avoided or ignored (Oliver, 1991) or buffered through decoupling (Meyer & Rowan, 1977). Triggers that are based on innovations that might be beneficial to some incumbent actors but disruptive to others are likely to be reframed or interpreted in a way that would lead to more congruent practice, form, or ideas (Westphal, Gulati, & Shortell, 1997).

These varying effects of triggers direct our examination to the role of attention and problematization. Organizations in many fields periodically handle small shocks or routine changes as part of their normal operations (March & Olsen, 1989), thus requiring minimal change. They rely primarily on built-in shifts in attention, problem-solving, and absorption as a form of learning and slow rule change through the normal encoding of experience (Cohen & Levinthal, 1990; March, Schulz & Zhou, 2000). Other larger and unexpected shocks demand more extensive efforts at theorization and absorption. Some of this theorization may appear to be rational, but often it is driven by institutional maintenance needs and a desire by some to reframe and categorize the nature of the shock as inconsequential (Perrow, 2007; Weick, 1993). The resulting absorption is often partial and may lead to suboptimal adjustment (Gavetti & Levinthal, 2000).

In a purely political reading of triggers and shocks, these efforts at identifying, framing, and channeling events become more evident. Organizational fields and the institutions within them are subject to dialectical forces of stasis and change (Benson, 1977) and often contain contradictions that cannot be ignored (Bourdieu, 1977; Seo & Creed, 2002). Triggers, as a result, are created or leveraged by different interest groups vying for power (Fligstein & McAdam, 2012). In what might be described as "institutional war," core and secondary elites, peripheral groups, and resisting camps vie for positions to gain more power and control (Bourdieu, 2011; Foucault, 1977). As an example of one category of shock, technological changes are filtered through power and interest, as can be seen by the efforts of workers in factories to control the introduction and application of new technologies (Gouldner, 1954). The ensuing negotiations and resorting of the field then leads to new temporary settlements until a new exogenous shock leads to internal contradictions and another round of engagement.

In our institutional-political variant, we agree that there are tensions in relational fields due to power asymmetries, complex logics, and competing institutions. But unless attention and other resources are focused on these asymmetries, the differences are unlikely to become contradictions that lead to power contests. Additionally, exogenous shocks from adjacent fields, whether social, technological, natural, or political, are likely to diffuse across boundaries, particularly when the adjacent fields are more tightly linked and overlapping. Yet the timing and meaning of those shocks will depend on the power structures and cultures of the focal field. Many shocks will lead to problematization and then to the routing of attention, resources, and mobilization along different paths. But the main paths are the technical (to scientific or managerial decision-making routes) or the political (to regulatory policy formation or bureaucratic negotiations). These two paths, as can be seen at the end of this section and in Section 4, are quite distinct in their institutional dynamics.

3.1.1 Triggers, Disruptive Events, and Cultural Anomalies in Anthropocene Society

Turning more specifically to the Anthropocene and the ecosystems views of shocks, one sees that shocks increase as thresholds are approached. These shocks reverberate through natural and social systems from the links or nodes in which they appear. Ideally, the extant tracking and problem-solving subsystems handle such events before they become too disruptive, or are slightly modified to do so. If they are not dampened, these shocks begin to cause subsystem disruption followed by wider failure. They also cascade to adjacent natural and social systems, causing cumulative disruption (Polhill et al., 2016; Rhodes, 2014). For example, sugar cane production in Brazil has experienced many exogenous weather and economic shocks that were initially dampened. But with political difficulties inside the country, these shocks have now become more disruptive to cane and biofuel production (Verstegen et al., 2016). Similarly, variances in hurricane strength and paths, something that has increased in recent years (Zandbergen, 2009), have made it difficult to isolate and repair the resultant damage. Some even argue that repair is no longer possible, which has forced a reevaluation of community and government approaches to rebuilding efforts (LeJeune, 2011).

In the social world of Anthropocene Society, this implies that these increasingly disruptive events will require even stronger filtering and interpretation. In our institutional-political view of institutions, incumbent power interests will spend ever greater amounts of time and resources trying to diminish the relevance of shocks, in large part by recoding them as routine events or the "new normal" so that they do not reach the level of disruption and begin cascading into other systems. Hurricanes, for instance, have been made into common news by some media channels that represent incumbent interests, where they are rated and tracked but then are left behind by most viewers and analysts as the next news item approaches (Holt, 2006). Recently, however, the succession of events is having a cumulative impact, particularly because the public pays attention to the ever-larger peaks, valleys, frequencies, and payouts. The contested views then become part of the war between frames of "exceeded planetary boundaries" versus "normal weather cycles," with the intermediate language and currency being familiar frames of jobs, the economy, government policy, infrastructure innovations, habitat loss, etc.

In Anthropocene Society, some events, such as the Deepwater Horizon disaster, become too large to frame as nondisruptive. These events serve as potential "cultural anomalies" (Hoffman & Jennings, 2011) that do not fit with existing legitimacy structures and compel changes in the deeper culture of Anthropocene Society. The cultural anomaly reverberates through the institutional system, moving from event to attention (Hoffman & Ocasio, 2001) at the micro-mezzo level, from sense-making to decision making to social mobilization at the macro level, and ultimately to new forms of rules and regulations, different approaches to risk, and the assignment of blame among specific field members (both for social sanctioning and scapegoating). But such events become truly disruptive only if they spill over into the institution or field-level operation at a fundamental level of culture. For example, in the case of the BP Deepwater Horizon disaster, activists sought to frame the event as anomalous by focusing on the extent to which the fossil-fuel culture that underlies all industrial economies leads to ever-riskier pursuits of available oil. While the event almost became a full-scale anomaly, the machinery of blame, payouts, and technological fixes eventually blunted any change. However, if a similar incident were to occur in the near future and be tied to oil and weather events, it would seem unlikely such social repair could occur without wider shifts in society's use of such oil.

3.1.2 Research Opportunities on Triggers, Disruptive Events, and Cultural Anomalies

The role of triggers and anomalous events offers rich areas for further research. For example, why are some cumulative events, such as ice shelf calvings and toxic spills, attended to as separate and discrete events, while others, such as hurricanes, are reframed as part of a class of events, often as normal and entertaining news? Other events, such as reactor breaches and oil spills, may still be disruptive, but more research is necessary for deeper assessment beyond descriptive mapping of the events. One interesting avenue of study, for instance, is the ways in which the discourses of weather and climate overlap and are parsed. The shift in discourse about the weather, from local to international, from the weather out the window to potentials on the statistical horizon, is one clue as to how the natural environment is apprehended and translated as a logic. Another important research topic is an examination of the balance between exogenous and endogenous triggers and how these are shifting over time through processes of construction. Hurricanes were historically considered to be exogenous to social systems. But in the new social order of Anthropocene Society, they become endogenous for the communities, corporations, and governments in their path or involved in relief efforts and most importantly, for elements of social systems that are the ultimate cause in their increased intensity and frequency through a changing climate.

3.2 Institutional Entrepreneurs and Social Mobilization

Mainstream institutional theories view institutional entrepreneurs as actors who are able to modify institutionalized ideas, practices, institutions, or fields (Hardy & Maguire, 2008; Jennings et al., 2011). Entrepreneurs do this wittingly or unwittingly through some degree of agency (choice, free will, or directed action). The definition of institutional entrepreneurship is less controversial than how they create change. For example, there is the paradox of embedded agency (Garud & Karnøe, 2003), in which the agent is both embedded in and shaped by the very field the agent is trying to use and modify. One solution to this paradox has been to examine micro-institutional work as a process through which an agent might create change (Lawrence et al., 2009). The process might involve reframing and then controlling change mechanisms through indirect means. Neither method would require that the agent be able to transcend the field while acting in it. A different solution has been to think of agency as more distributed in a relational field, and thus allowing constellations of actors and processes to work in concert to create change (Rao, Monin, & Durand, 2003). This type of distributed agency frequently involves joint mobilization. As such, it may rely directly on creating social movements to leverage them for the entrepreneurs' benefit (Lounsbury, Ventresca, & Hirsch, 2003).

In a more political reading of entrepreneurship (after all, entrepreneurship is, by definition, political), we see less of a focus on specific actors than on *habitus* and *praxis* (Bourdieu & Wacquant, 1992; Lawrence et al., 2009). Actors enact and reproduce social relations and field structure via habitus; but that enactment is rarely perfect, nor are the field relations without contradictions. More mindful or focused action on the part of some groups, based around their field position and forms of capital, creates more explicit change to a new form of praxis reflecting power and social relations. This new form then modifies the field itself.

The model of entrepreneurship within the notion of SAFs has an even more explicit focus on actors as strategic agents – whether incumbents or challengers – that use their social skills and toolkits to pursue specific goals (Fligstein & McAdam, 2012). The skills are based on "cognitive, affective, and linguistic faculties" (Fligstein & McAdam, 2012: 46) and are aimed at using either authority or persuasion to induce cooperation. When authority is used, power, domination, and coercion are central elements of field-level change. When persuasion is used, it is arranged through appeals to shared meaning, collective identity (Bourdieu, 1977), and framing (Goffman, 1974). Not surprisingly, in this SAF version of entrepreneurship, social movements can also be created or leveraged by actors to generate change.

In our institutional-political variant, institutional entrepreneurship builds on these views. Agency may be focused on one actor or may be distributed, but it relies heavily on social skills and mobilization that enables action. However, many entrepreneurial endeavors fail and social movements end before achieving their goals. While such aborted change efforts may raise key issues to the collective attention level, the effects are only temporary, as the efforts are absorbed into the normal operations of the field or institution, or are forgotten after the issue-attention cycle is over (Downs, 1972). Should structures of status and domination, which underlie many fields, be directly threatened by such changes, force will be used against the entrepreneurs and social movement members in an effort to silence their voices.

Another critical observation is that institutional entrepreneurs and social movements today, more than ever, require both tangible and intangible resources (Jasper, 2010). Entrepreneurs are able to be bricoleurs, but bricolage requires that components are readily available for assembly (Hardy & Maguire, 2008). However, in the modern economy, incumbents work to reduce slack and waste, and attack or appropriate anything recognized as useful to other agents. So, having some resources in the first place becomes more important. Social analysts, such as those studying the Occupy Movement, Tea Party, or Arab Spring, have viewed virtual resources as more spontaneously generated and fungible (Castells, 2015) but also more evanescent and contested than ever before. So, controlling virtual resources seems more, not less, important in the emerging context of our social media world.

Institutional entrepreneurship, therefore, is best carried out less directly and more collaboratively through multiple methods. One method is through innovation – creating particular new practices or proto-forms through local experiments (hopefully with others' resources), which can then be absorbed into the field at lower cost to the innovating actors and incumbents (Lawrence et al., 2002). Another method is through the exploitation of triggers, anomalies, or disruptive events, framed as solutions rather than problems. This will attract resources and attention and move a group forward (Schussler, Ruling, & Wittneben, 2014). A third method is to shift debate by introducing "radical flank effects" and shift the center of field-level debate, thereby bringing previously peripheral issues into mainstream discourse (Schifeling & Hoffman, 2017). Finally, a fourth method is to find or create iconic leaders who look and act in authentic ways on the group's behalf. Today, social movements engage with known or recognizable figureheads through social media, but the exacting nature of that media requires that these leaders act without compromise (Castells, 2015). Any deviation from the message of the movement will be instantly captured and distributed (go "viral"), inducing planetary scorn.

3.2.1 Institutional Entrepreneurs and Social Mobilization in the Anthropocene

In the Anthropocene, central nodes become brokerage points that are increasingly important for maintaining subsystems. These points might, for example, be key stocks in the food chain, key bodies of seasonally refreshed water, or key economic actors in the carbon-reliant production and consumption markets. There is also increasing complexity and uncertainty in the decisions of entrepreneurs stemming from combining multiple types of decisions (economic, political, social) with the need to balance competing interests, and allocate tangible and intangible resources at a time when these resources are becoming more scarce and dispersed in the system. Consequently, the strategies of politically astute entrepreneurs must be leveraged at key nodes in the systems of Anthropocene Society.

For example, the set of nodes that surround and link issues related climate change and maximum carbon production, such as particular regions, states, corporations, and ENGOs become locales. These are the nodes where regulatory frameworks and budgets for carbon conversion are formed and where action is coordinated. The US coal and fracking districts in Pennsylvania and Canada's Oil Sands stand as specific instances where film makers, musician activists, ENGOs, and local politicians have become entrepreneurs promoting institutional change (Misutka et al., 2013).

Indirect, distributed entrepreneurial action will also be necessary at each of these nodes through innovation, the exploitation of triggers, the introduction of radical flanks, and the clear presence of iconic leadership to generate change. For example, concerns over climate change, elevated by recent storms such as Hurricane Maria in Puerto Rico, have elevated voices for shifting the focus of the debate toward more acceptance of renewable energy, energy storage, electric vehicles, driverless vehicles, and the continued demise of oil and coal as energy sources. Additionally, each of these shifts has been accompanied by leverage at governmental nodes (city, state, and federal), activating credit financing and benefit from government defined (if partially deregulated) markets (Joo et al., 2017; Russo, 2003; Sine & Lee, 2009).

Some have argued that the transnational nature of the planetary boundaries of the Anthropocene and their interconnected and overlapping nature require entrepreneurs and social movements at multiple scales and scope, most notably transnational organizations and their representatives that can act in concert with national and local groups to initiate efforts for change at multiple scales (Davis & Zald, 2005). But it is not clear whether the existing ecosystem of social movements will merely revert to the historic pattern of multistakeholder negotiated frameworks (Espeland, 1998) or develop new forms and structures for resolving novel transnational issues. The outcome of gentle change often resembles the incremental (and therefore insufficient) change efforts of the past (Schussler, Ruling, & Wittneben, 2014) though there are active experiments to see if such groups can be coordinated for more radical and transformational change.

3.2.2 Research Opportunities on Institutional Entrepreneurs and Social Mobilization

Numerous opportunities lie in the area of institutional entrepreneurship as it relates to the Anthropocene. Building on a rich and vibrant research tradition, one area is the study of who has voice in theorizing the constellation of events that emerge within the Anthropocene for maximum effect. Each frame used by entrepreneurs triggers a different set of actors. For example, hurricanes, which are reported by weather people (announcers, analysts, and meteorologists) draw general public attention, but that attention dissipates quickly. Forest fires, on the other hand, are the domain of mainstream news as well as state and federal agencies which focus local community attention and tend to remain stable through rebuilding efforts.

A second area for study is around the tools and tactics employed by entrepreneurs. Many fields of the Anthropocene are just forming or maturing. Therefore, significant skill is focused on pulling together disparate groups and chaining their concerns to create proto-organizations, which resemble either a recognized form (i.e., B Corporations) or a social movement (Gehman, Trevino, & Garud, 2013). Whether these actions should rely on emotional appeals, logics, or teleological claims is an open question.

A third area is to examine new forms of social movement. The remote locations of many Anthropocene events (i.e., the Artic, the deep ocean, or the tropical jungle) mean that movements around these events must rely on social media and virtual organization. Yet the effervescent nature of movements created by such links (Jasper, 2010) also means that we need to research their "stickiness." These may be movements that glom onto corporations, government agencies, and foundations, and thus have more endurance and the power of resurgence when Anthropocene shocks occur.

3.3 Regulatory Change and Change Agents

Mainstream institutional theory has a long tradition of studying models of political decision making (March & Olsen, 1989; Selznick, 1949) and political bureaucracies (Allison, 1971; Selznick, 1949), especially within formal institutionalism (North, 1991; Williamson, 1985), and political institutionalism (Krasner, 1988; March & Olsen, 1989). Consistent with its importance, Scott's (1995) overview of institutional theory gives the regulatory pillar specific prominence in the three pillars of institutionalism. In fact, in his treatment of institutional dynamics, no analysis is complete without consideration of the state.

In more current models of institutionalism, this regulatory pillar has been expressed in different components, but not considered in such an evident way as in Scott's earlier work. In the streams on micro-level logics and attention (Thornton, Ocasio, & Lounsbury, 2012), there is focus on political decision making and negotiations that percolate up to the field level often, but not always, as laws, rules, and policies. Whether such macro-level instruments of control become more salient depends on the extent to which the field involves state-based logics. In the streams on institutional complexity (Greenwood et al., 2011), regulatory processes are expressed through field centralization and organizational governance, both parts of all fields though they do not necessarily guide institutional change. Regardless, complexity research often has an eye to such mechanisms, as can been seen in work on the formation of new human resource practices in law and accounting (Smets et al., 2012).

In political and critical theory readings of institutional operation, regulatory processes are far more central. The historical evolution of key fields, such as markets and professions, depends on the rise and involvement of the state (Foucault, 2007). In such fields, bureaucratic functionaries are able to define constituents, set boundaries (territory), and link both to processes of security. Regulatory power itself emerges in different forms to maintain conformity among field members, such as domination, which is deeper and more objectified, and discipline, which is more overt and subjective (Lawrence & Buchanan, 2017; Lawrence et al., 2001). These power dynamics are generally reinforced through the application or threat of force and violence (Foucault, 1977). Bourdieu (2011) while Bourdieu and Wacquant (1992) soften this version of power and regulation by making it more cultural and relational within the context of fields. Regulation may be based on political approaches and political capital, but social and cultural capital underpins the ways that field relations are expressed.

In contrast, the SAF translation of these principles offers strong endorsement of the centrality of the state and governance as key features of fields.

> SAFs have formal governance units that are charged with overseeing compliance with field rules and, in general, facilitating the overall smooth functioning of the system. It is important to note that these units are internal to the field and distinct from external state structures that hold jurisdiction over all, or some aspect of, the SAF. (Fligstein & McAdam, 2011: 6)

In our institutional-political variant, fields are relational with large amounts of vertically structured power. There are many substantively important institutions and organizations, which are the key institutional actors. Change processes based on triggers are leveraged by entrepreneurs or social movements. Both domination and discipline are also present, with episodic uses of power, typically experienced directly through influence and rules at multiple levels (such as municipal, regional, national, and international), but often observed indirectly as force or its threat. The presence of the state within fields is embodied in individuals who are its representatives, either as regulators, auditors, or liaisons with state powers. These "regulatory agents," in the broadest sense, help articulate state power and, more specifically, its laws, rules, and policies. The state and its regulators have been viewed in political theory and in some areas of institutionalism as primarily conservative preservers of stability and maintenance of the status quo.

However, the state and its functionaries also have their own agendas that go beyond the maintenance of corporate or community interests (Pedriana & Stryker, 2004). As a result, regulatory agents can be seen as change agents pursuing multiple interests. Among these interests might be the enlargement and enhancement of the state machinery that empowers the agent (Colignon, 1997; Downs, 1967). Work has also shown that well-placed political functionaries may be important for changing the underlying logic of a system, for example, from a technical to a bureaucratic orientation (Baron, Dobbin, & Jennings, 1986). More recently, work on economic adaptation and technological entrepreneurship in China has shown the importance of having government officials tied to boards or to owners of firms in order to help clear the path for investment (Gedajlovic, Cao, & Zhang, 2012).

3.3.1 Regulatory Change and Change Agents in the Anthropocene

In ecosystems theory, complex systems require key regulatory processes and decisions to maintain balance (Palsson et al., 2013). For instance, growth loops, population distribution loops, and food chains require balancing mechanism for the preservation of the ecosystem (Galaz, 2012). In more chaos-based or rapid evolution variants of ecosystem theory, some form of temporary equilibrium is created through self-organization within a combination of subsystems.

In the Anthropocene Era, the impact of such regulatory processes and regulatory nodes is weakened. Population, consumption and other growth loops are reinforced, which accelerate resource use. Economic entities become more engaged across boundaries through trade and factor flows, increasing coordination problems. The amount of waste and pollution increases commensurately, and there are more frequent and severe trigger events due to temporary systems collapses (or efforts to recalibrate).

Not surprisingly, Anthropocene Society requires increased regulatory involvement at all levels. Regulatory policies are necessary to deal with climate change, resource overuse, and peak events such as hurricanes and forest fires (Hackler, 2011; Marcus, Aragon-Correa, & Pinkse, 2011; Whiteman, Walker,

& Perego, 2013). But, on average, the nation-state is weaker now than in the past fifty years (Davis & Zald, 2005). Regulatory agents are blocked by process demands (Perrow, 2007; Vogel, 1996), and the effects of their laws and policies are becoming more ephemeral or heavily deflected by translation (Dobbin, 2009). So, while there is a need for regulatory involvement at all levels, it seems unlikely to be commensurate with the growing ecological needs of the Anthropocene.

Fortunately, there are some Anthropocene fields, communities, and issues where this is less true. For example, renewable energy production is one area where government intervention has supported market and technological development. In the United States, renewable energy has increased to 15 percent of total energy production (when hydropower is included), due in part to regulatory support. Renewables in Germany are reaching more than 27 percent of energy production and may reach more than 80 percent by 2050 (Kunzig, 2015). China installed more solar capacity in 2016 than any other country and has announced aggressive targets for renewables for 2050 (Ball et al., 2017). Similarly, the growing markets for electric and hybrid vehicle use have also increased with the support of regulatory interventions. While these changes may not be sufficient to fully address climate change, they are important.

There are also some specific regulatory change agents who have more power to coordinate complex fields and encourage collaborative (or require coercively mandated) solutions. As a state, China is now considered to be ahead in taking forceful, focused action on several climate issues, even to the point of shutting factories when national leaders meet, if partly out of embarrassment about the related pollution (*Economist*, 2017b). India has set equally stringent targets, at the very moment when the United States has withdrawn its commitment and stewardship in this area. The United Nations has been considered a legitimate body for adjudicating environmental disputes, though its ability to act has been curtailed in part by its unwieldy governance structure. The World Bank, while ostensibly a market-based institution, has many effects on environmental management (such as waste management) through its lending practices that require good environmental practice as monitored by auditors.

3.3.2 Research Opportunities on Regulatory Change and Change Agents

The area of government policy for the Anthropocene is an area that would benefit from institutional scholarship. The forms of appropriate interventions into markets, the types of technology fostered, and the corporations favored are all areas of a research program on organizational politics and regulation that go beyond standard notions of cartel or corporate capture, to models where government actors (i.e., agencies, parties, lobbyists) work in more co-equal (competitive and collaborative) fashion with other organizational actors. This research stream might investigate the indirect effects of government policy and interventions, including multimodal, multidomain roles for governments on different Anthropocene boundaries. For examples, government action on renewables in Scandinavian, American, Asian, and African countries can reveal deep insights into the form and politics of policy implementation in multiple contexts. This work could then be extended to an assessment of similar policy implementation at the transnational level. Further, institutional scholars might benefit from studying government actors as regulatory change agents. They are not simply entrepreneurs, but driven by the need to maintain as well as change, represent, and create new structures. Ties to these agents may benefit field actors as forms of political capital whose effects can be studied.

3.4 Conclusion

In this section, we have modified institutional theory further by examining three sets of institutional change mechanisms. We have done so by amending mainstream institutional approaches with contributions from political and systems theory as they apply to the Anthropocene as summarized in Table 2. In the next section, we will complete our development of an institutional-political model by turning to two cross-cutting issues that relate to the powerful counterculture that resists Anthropocene science, policy and belief.

4 Resistance from Countercultures Denying Anthropocene Issues

In this section, we delve more deeply into the resistance and skepticism that emerges from countercultures that deny Anthropocene problems. This is a powerful component of the social movement dynamics in Anthropocene Society, as the highly contentious debate over climate change makes vivid. By challenging the wide-ranging and critical domains of science, authority, evidence, facts, values, and physical phenomena, the skeptics have tried to shift the fundamental human relationship with the natural environment (Hoffman, 2015; Hulme, 2009). This brings us back to the consideration of how the natural and social sciences can be combined to understand our emergent reality (Weber, 1949).

Table 2. Amendments to Institutional Theory Change Mechanisms in Light of the Anthropocene

Theoretical Mechanisms	Political-Institutional Variant	Application to Anthropocene Society
Disruptive events and cultural anomalies	Disruptive events increase in frequency and interdependency, becoming constellations. Incumbent power interests attempt to minimize their import if they challenge their legitimacy and have them accepted as "the new normal." In other words, they work to assure that event constellations do not become cultural anomalies that trigger change.	Previously understood events need new theorizing and problematizing in the new context of the Anthropocene. For example, what is weather and what is climate change? Constellations of events, such as repeated hurricanes or droughts, need to be linked to make sense and be translated into other logics and fields. Cultural anomalies must be cultivated. More cumulative disruptions affect bases of power within the field.
Institutional entrepreneurs and social mobilization	Cultural entrepreneurs define and leverage disruptive events and the interests of actors. They overcome resistance in order to change field dynamics and disrupt specific institutions.	ENGOs, scientific agencies, government actors, and emergent industries (i.e., renewable energy) compete within field-level debates with incumbent industries (i.e., fossil fuels), and skeptical political, ideological, and economic groups to define Anthropocene events and issues.

| Regulatory change and regulatory change agents | Fields are relational and structured (especially vertically) around power. Hence, degrees of domination and discipline exist alongside more collaborative, symmetric arrangements. Regulatory actors (such as the state) and their agents are in most fields (and their own social order) where they seek to reinforce the status quo for cultural elites, but they also have their own agendas for pushing change. | Regulatory rules and regulatory agents are considered essential, but are often difficult to create and not comprehensive enough in the various transnational Anthropocene fields. Some institutional actors, such as the UN and World Bank, and some states, for example, Germany and China, have made significant changes in their own actions and, as a result, within broader fields. |

4.1 The Climate Change Field and New Counterculture

Scientific communities (i.e., the US National Academy of Sciences) and many cultural groups (i.e., democratic politicians, ENGOs, etc.) have adopted a dominant institutional logic that Anthropogenic climate change is real and in need of attention. However, institutions inherently contain contradictions and multiple logics are often available to individuals and organizations as they operate within them (Friedland & Alford, 1991). This means that along with the dominant logic that climate change is a serious problem warranting action, there also exists a challenger logic (Bertels, Hoffman, & DeJordy, 2014; McAdam & Scott, 2005) that asserts that climate change is not a problem at all (Hoffman, 2011). These challenger logics often strike deeply discordant messages and apply tactics to disrupt social debate. For example, US Senator James Inhofe has called climate change "the greatest hoax ever perpetrated on the American people" and think tanks (such as the Heartland Institute) and corporations (such as Exxon-Mobil) have sought to deliberately confuse the presentation of science on this issue.

We are in what Kuhn (1962) refers to as "revolutionary science," a period of flux when an anomalous event or issue challenges the dominant order. More specifically, we are in a period in which an understanding of the Anthropocene and its prominent marker, climate change, is not yet fully formed and its possible solutions have not yet been fully resolved, despite perspectives within the academy that it has. As a challenge to the existing economic and political order has emerged through its articulation, conflicts and tensions between competing logics are brought to the surface through framing debates and discursive contests. The domain in which these challenges are resolved can be described as an institutional "field of struggles" (Bourdieu & Wacquant, 1992) where competing logics are presented and promoted for dominance in describing the emergent and accepted conception of reality.

To help us understand the form and dynamics of this challenger movement of skeptics and the resistance they create for institutional debates, we turn to our institutional-political variant and its application to Anthropocene Society. Though organizational inertia has been a traditional marker of field level institutional debates (Zucker, 1983), our political reading treats inertia as politically inflected, where organizations and individuals mount concerted efforts to promote or resist change based on their particular interests (Fiss & Hirsch, 2005). Because the notion of the Anthropocene can be competency and status enhancing for some and destroying for others, the topic and its associated markers are highly controversial with lines drawn along economic, ideological, and political lines. To examine these phenomena further, we will consider two specific institutional elements – the (dis)engagement of constituencies and their local logics and cultures – and then turn to the change mechanisms that are (dis)engaged. We complete the section with a discussion of research opportunities.

4.1.1 Constituencies (Dis)Engaged

Inertia may emerge from resistance groups that include those that are conversely advantaged or disadvantaged by the introduction of new concepts or notions of reality. In the social debate over climate change, proponents on one side may include affected communities (i.e., small island states), scientific agencies (i.e., IPCC, US National Academy of Sciences), nonprofit organizations (i.e., WWF), and new entrant corporate groups (i.e., those representing new and alternative forms of energy). Opponents on the other side may include incumbent corporate groups (i.e., the fossil-fuel industry and US Chamber of Commerce) and conservative think tanks (i.e., the Heartland Institute, Cato Institute, Competitive Enterprise Institute) (Hoffman, 2015). This latter category is highly organized and has been labeled as the "climate change counter movement," made up of nearly 100 organizations that oppose climate policy (Brulle, 2014).

Engagement between these opposing movements creates ideological and cultural influences on discursive debates – or framing battles – over the interpretation of the problem and the necessity and nature of solutions (Hoffman, 2011). In this battle, embedded values around a complex array of issue categories related to religion, economics, risk, freedom, national security, and others are engaged (Hulme, 2009). Thus, these competing groups manifest themselves into ideological positions, which in turn influence the competing frames with which particular issues and events are represented and debated. Competition among these competing definitions form a kind of institutional "war" that ensues, and ultimately results in shifts in embedded institutions, specific practices, and economic or political fortunes of those engaged. In the field of struggles that emerges, those embracing the dominant logic set the rules of the game, and challengers seek to change those rules by replacing dominant principles and actions with logics of their own. The outcomes of such contests have wide-ranging implications for society and social structure, often creating new policy domains and new market segments (Weber, Heinze, & DeSoucey, 2008).

4.1.2 Local Political Logics and Cultures (Dis)Engaged

An examination of counter movements of resistance and skepticism towards climate change involves a consideration for the kinds of competing logics that are brought to bear, that is, the contrary ideas and belief systems with a particular focus on "the role they play in providing direction, motivation, meaning and coherence" (McAdam & Scott, 2005: 16). These logics go well beyond the direct issue at hand and may include a belief that climate science and climate policy are a covert way for liberal environmentalists and the government to interfere in the market and diminish citizens' personal freedom; a strong faith in the free market and a resistance to legislation that will hinder economic progress; and a strong distrust of scientific institutions and the scientific peer review process (Hoffman, 2011). For some, a belief in climate change even threatens their belief in God and leads to a rejection of any notion that humans have become so powerful that they can alter the global climate (Hoffman, 2015).

One strand of research explores how resistance is, in part, reflected in political affiliation and values, with the predominance of US conservatives rejecting an acceptance of climate change and the preponderance of liberals accepting it (McCright & Dunlap, 2011). Conservatives tend to support "system justification" and a motivational tendency to defend and justify the status quo. Consistent with a capitalist market logic, those who employ this logic will be skeptical of environmental risks as such beliefs would justify restricting the free-market economy and individual freedom and responsibility, values that they feel are threatened by an acceptance of climate change (Feygina, Jost, & Goldsmith, 2010). As such, resistance to climate change is often aligned with relatively hierarchical and individualistic values in the United States. Conversely, the logic of those who believe in climate change is aligned with more egalitarian and communitarian values. Those who employ this logic will be inclined to accept environmental risks because they resent unrestrained commerce and self-interested behavior and readily accept that such activities are dangerous and worthy of regulation (Douglas & Wildavsky, 1982; Kahan, Jenkins-Smith, & Braman, 2010; Rayner, 1992).

Hierarchical groups tend to perceive industrial and technological risks as opportunities and thus less risky, whereas more egalitarian groups tend to perceive them as threats to their social structure (Weber, 2006). Consistent with this view, US conservatives report significantly less trust in science that identifies environmental and public health impacts of economic production and more trust in science that provides new innovations that support economic production (McCright et al., 2013). Climate change challenges the great trust they have that market forces will lead to positive ends (Vargish, 1980). Oreskes and Conway (2010) catalogued these ideological themes and show how they are linked with those at play in the US campaigns over cigarette smoking and lung cancer, coal smoke and acid rain, and chlorofluorocarbon (CFCs) and the ozone hole. They also note that some of the same people and organizations were involved in each of these issues and that they were staunchly anticommunist and extremely supportive of free markets as the key to their world views with near religious fervor. Other studies show a strong correlation between support for free-market ideology and rejection of climate science (Heath & Gifford, 2006), as well as the rejection of other established scientific findings, such as the facts that HIV caused AIDS, and that smoking causes lung cancer (Lewandowsky, Oberauer, & Gignac, 2013).

More recent studies have found that the partisan dimension of the climate debate is still fluid, with surveys (Clear Path, 2015) showing that 54 percent of self-described conservative Republicans in the United States now believe that the world's climate is changing and that mankind plays some role in the change. Nevertheless, the debate over climate change science and the notion of the Anthropocene remains contested within the United States and will continue to reach levels that are more foundational to the multiple logics that structure our society (as noted by its challenge to religion and belief in God). This is an outcome that is consistent with the paradigm shifting nature of the Anthropocene Era, and one that renders its emergence as uniquely disruptive as a new institutional order.

4.1.3 Disruption as Change Mechanism (Dis)Engaged?

Institutional logics tend to create shared worldviews and frames that are then used to present and articulate events and their meaning. At the same time, such events may cause disruptions in such logics, leading to new cultural frames that become particularly salient with groups that seek change (McAdam & Scott, 2005), allowing for the mobilization of a movement and lending structure and organization to a set of specific practices (Swidler, 1986; Weber, Heinze, & DeSoucey, 2008). As such, the interpretation and even simple acknowledgment of specific events becomes highly contentious among movement and countermovement members in various organizational fields.

For example, hurricanes in the Caribbean, droughts in the American southwest, and wildfires in the American west have been common occurrences throughout history. Yet, more recent storms, droughts, and wildfires have hit areas of economic or political importance with greater force and frequency than has been historically typical. One interpretation within the United States is that these events are within the natural bounds of natural variability. Another interpretation is that they represent a step change to the increasingly destructive outcomes of human-induced climate change. Each interpretation yields responses that are economically, ideologically, and politically contested with various field-level constituencies. What kind of government intervention is warranted, and to what degree? What kinds of rebuilding efforts will be under-taken – those that represent past practices or new construction models that plan for these storms to grow in severity? And what kinds of energy infrastructure will be developed? Will it be based on the fossil-fuel power plans that were destroyed, or new renewable energy sources and storage capacities?

Given such institutional complexity and meaning, those who resist action will squelch any attempts at social debate about the event's meaning. In the wake of the 2017 devastation to Houston from Hurricane Harvey and Puerto Rico from Hurricane Maria, some called for an acknowledgment that these were related to climate change while others sought to dismiss such recognition; the US EPA administrator Scott Pruitt, acting as a regulatory agent, argued that talking about climate change during hurricanes is "very, very insensitive," only further attesting to the highly contentious and political nature of Anthropocene climate change events. The ability to ignore such events in the Anthropocene and to avert attention away from their consideration is a very worrisome pattern, given the core scientific models of the Anthropocene revolve around PBs and concerted action.

4.1.4 Research Opportunities on Resistance from Counter-Cultures

To date, there has been limited research on the actual constituencies of climate change resistance and the mechanisms they use to disruptive institutional debate; there has been even less on Anthropocene resistance. This mirrors a longstanding problem in social movement theory which for decades has not attended enough to politically conservative movements, although this has begun to change (see Blee & Creasap, 2010). Cooter (2013) for example, conducted in-person interviews of the militia and anti-government movements in Michigan, examining how members respond to changing ideas about equal-ity and inclusion while belonging to a group that holds onto a vision of the nation where white men had exclusive social power. More of this kind of research is necessary as it is problematic to sample on the dependent variable and examine debates among groups that already agree that solutions to climate change are necessary. As the election of President Trump and the decision by the United Kingdom to exit the European Union make clear, we need to attend to those opposed (and indifferent) to social change in order to understand the landscape of the Anthropocene debate more completely.

A second opportunity for research is around the study of the nature of scientific truth and its standing in Anthropocene Society. This research agenda would include an examination of the ways in which the truths and roles of scientists are a reflection of the different political logics in which they derive, argue for, and implement their truths (Lefsrud & Meyer, 2012; Thornton, Ocasio & Lounsbury, 2012). The logic of science and technology makes the pursuit of truth less problematic, and truths established by method, less challenged on fundamentals. The derivation of truths and the verification of them in other logics and fields is not the same. For example, in religion, truth is known via canon and spiritual reflection. Such a method and the derived outcomes are normally viewed as invalid and unreliable within science (Popper, 1956). Instead, it would seem more effective to have religious groups engage with science truths and methods, then work to some common points. The Papal Encyclical, *Laudato Si,* for example (Pope Francis, 2015) offered reflections of the Pope, after consultation with both scientific and other leaders, on the role of humans as planetary stewards – a point of great agreement with Anthropocene scientists. This would seem a place from which to build even more positive understanding and action.

4.2 Conclusion

In this section, we have completed our examination and amendments to our institutional-political variant of institutional theory by focusing on resistance from within the counterculture to Anthropocene Society. Our hope is that social and physical scientists will engage on the various fields and communities related to the Anthropocene. However, we recognize that more holistic and comprehensive approaches must be taken if we are to shift our production, consumption, and appreciation within Anthropocene Society. With that in mind, we next turn our lens toward examining different institutional archetypes – holistic pictures for what Anthropocene Society might look like.

5 Three Archetypes of Anthropocene Society: Collapsed Systems, Market Rules, and Technology Fix

The examination of countercultures to climate change that exist in many organizational fields in Anthropocene Society and the various means of disengagement leads the researcher and reader to wonder about other knock-on consequences of Anthropocene Society. What has been the result of this contestation in the various fields aside from the creation of inertia and the blocking of progress in dealing with Anthropocene issues? Based on our institutional-political reading of these fields, we see that some degree of balkanization has occurred about the nature of Anthropocene issues. But we also see that there appears to be different views about possible ways to deal with climate, biodiversity and other Anthropocene issues among specific individuals and groups within different fields. Indeed, the viewpoints have particular features that lead us to label them "archetypes."

Archetypes are defined as ideal form depictions of a social unit's values and actions. They are based on conceptual properties about the social unit and allow for the meaning (intended or not) of the group to be understood (Weber, 1949). Archetypes are thus social scientific tools to help observers understand how social actors' views of the world guide behavior. They are used, in particular, when "direct understanding" of behavior due to prior conceptual and actor-specific information, such as conditions, motives, and causal nexuses, is not available (Weber, 1949). That behavior may take place at work, at home, in spiritual life, or elsewhere.

In organization theory, an archetype is more specifically "a set of structures and systems that consistently embodies a single interpretive scheme" (Greenwood & Hinings, 1993: 1055). As such, archetypes sit between general and specific knowledge and between hypothesis and historical observation. They are also an expression of deeper cultural myths and tendencies that tend to manifest themselves in different specific ways, but rely on an underlying form (Jung, 2014). For instance, a century ago, Max Weber (1958) demonstrated, quite counterintuitively, that the archetypical Protestant Ethic of hard work and saving in communities and business, which adherents hoped would lead them to heaven, aligned with archetypical capitalist behavior of investing, innovating, and exploring new markets. These disparate archetypes helped Weber to determine both how and why Protestant colonies helped spread capitalism to the New World, something that, on the surface, seemed paradoxical.

Today, when examining the growing discussions and understanding of the Anthropocene among different social actors, we see four different archetypes that appear to be possible for typifying that discourse and the approaches to action: Collapsed Systems, Market Rules, Technology Fix, and Cultural Re-Enlightenment. These four represent a structured spectrum of possibilities that span between "worlds of calamitous discontinuity, and worlds of progressive transformation" (Raskin, 2014). The former is dystopian and we call it "Collapsed Systems"; the latter is utopian and we call it "Cultural Re-Enlightenment." In between, we might have "worlds of incremental adjustment" (Raskin, 2014) based on dominant logics, which we offer as "Market Rules" and "Technology Fix." This archetypal typology is also in keeping with what Raskin (2014) called "decline, progression and evolution" or "Barbarization, Great Transitions, and Conventional Worlds." We build on Raskin's typology by applying our political-institutional variant of institutional theory. To be consistent with our own institutional-political variant, we will apply the same set of elements and change mechanisms presented in Tables 1 and 2. We will present the Collapsed Systems, Market Rules, and Technology Fix archetypes in this section, and give special and more detailed attention to Cultural Re-Enlightenment in the next section.

5.1 The Collapsed Systems Archetype

Several groups of scientists, social scientists, and popular writers believe we are in a period of collapse (Rhodes, 2014). As Elizabeth Kolbert (2014: 3) notes:

> No creature has ever altered life on the planet this way before, and yet other comparable events have occurred. Very, very occasionally in the distant past, the planet has undergone change so wrenching that the diversity of life has plummeted. While it is too early to say whether it will reach the proportion of the Big Five, it becomes known as the Sixth Extinction.

According to the logics of this archetype, as represented by these writers, humans will likely survive the sixth extinction, but like all prior peak species facing great extinctions, they will be greatly stressed in the process. The effects on human society have been documented in other case studies of population-ecosystems collapse, such as in Easter Island, Greenland, Central America, and New Guinea (Diamond, 2005) and in great disruptions, like plagues (Diamond, 1999; Tuchman, 1979). In many such societal extinctions, the majority of animal species were lost, land was degraded, and local waters destroyed; in plagues, such as the bubonic plagues of fourteenth-century Europe, up to half of the population perished and many communities, farms, and tended hunting grounds disappeared.

Put in institutional terms, the logics underlying the Collapsed System archetype are dominated by a laissez-faire approach to market exchange with the goal of perpetual market (economic) growth. This cultural viewpoint may be reflected in a field of struggles in which one particular form of market logic dominates other logics that may offer some form of restraint or control. Many groups think of this as capitalism as denoted with a capital "C" (Kukel, 2017). In this archetype, the vector of unbridled production times consumption times population drives resource use and ecological damage to extreme outcomes (Sachs, 2008). There are very few rules to constrain this dynamic and even fewer to address its negative spillover effects. The more benevolent form, "neo-liberalism," includes some notion of the representative state, but suffers from similar problems.

The logics and institutions used to define Anthropocene events in Collapsed Systems will mark them as "normal" and simply within the bounds of historic weather patterns and natural variability. As such, most of the public will be only slightly aware of any specific environmental problems, whereas the benefits of environmental resource use causing those problems is concentrated among elites controlling business and capturing the government's interest. In circumstances when problems are more pronounced for the wider public, they still lack sufficient power to voice their concerns and neo-liberal based governments are unable to respond adequately to environmental issues (Vogel, 1996). As such, efforts to address Anthropocene issues will be framed simply as restraints on economic growth, which maintains the interests of elites and dissipates efforts at redress. As long as the elites of society remain unaffected by Anthropocene impacts, the status quo will be successfully defended and maintained.

Though the "C"apitalist market dominates, the organizational field within Collapsed Systems is fragmented. The logics of science are marginalized, with large and empowered countermovements enjoying a powerful voice in rejecting scientific analysis that points to a recognition of the Anthropocene. Not surprisingly, the most powerful institutions and change agents within the organizational field are those working on the capitalist market's behalf. Corporations that stand to lose from any attempt to recognize or address Anthropocene issues will hold great control over the content, form, and participation within institutional debates. Regulatory agents are muted such that the United Nations and the US EPA are no longer powerful in this archetype, compared to the International Monetary Fund, the World Bank, and the Federal Reserve (Harvey, 1990; Klein, 2001). These organizations discipline and develop regions – particularly emerging ones – using market principles. Transnational market-based groups, such as Sovereign Wealth Funds, and philanthropic-based groups, such as the Gates Foundation, are derived from market outcomes, pursuing clean-up and social initiatives primarily as an apologist for the dominant system, but without affecting Anthropocene dimensions in any substantive way (Wright & Nyberg, 2015).

The weakest actors in the field are the nonelites, those lacking financial or political means for market access and property ownership. These actors have limited recourse in Collapsed Systems to use social movements or countermovements for changing institutional discourse and structures. Various efforts, such as antinuclear or anti-GMO movements (Jasper, 2014) and the Green Party movement of the new millennium (Gray, Purdy, & Ansari, 2015), have only very limited electoral impact in only a few northern European states, with decreasing impact over time.

The only real restraint on the market logic of the Collapsed Systems archetype comes from nonmarket communities such as those in the religious and the nonprofit domains. But their impact is quite limited when faced with the dominant actors of the market and its co-opted regulatory structures. The Papal encyclical *Laudato Si* (Pope Francis, 2015) garnered some attention for a time and offered a clear critique of capitalism, but attention has dissipated, at least for the moment, and action has returned to business as usual. In the end, Collapsed Systems is marked by a continuation and escalation of the logics that created the Anthropocene issues in the first place, despite signals that they are creating calamitous results.

In the end, the predominant form of market logic diffuses through all domains of the Collapsed Systems archetype, moving not only into the state's domain and logic, but also into dominance over other spheres of social life – professions, communities, and religion. Through its spread, this logic variant of capitalism homogenizes culture – something once labelled "imperialism" (Harvey, 1990) and now more frequently "globalization" (Klein, 2001) – such that the trust and relational contracts used in traditional communities are replaced by transactional versions of exchange based primarily on monetary value as trumping all other measures of value (Peng & Heath, 1996). Any movement that counters the pursuit of economic growth will be thwarted.

5.2 The Market Rules Archetype

In this archetype of Anthropocene Society, the market again dominates institutional structures of society. But, unlike the prior one, the field is far more stabilized and the market logic is tempered by counter logics that lead to a hybrid form (Powell, 1987) that believes that the market, if properly guided, will solve many environmental problems. This, in many ways, is a continuation of the corporate sustainability logics of the market that emerged in the late twentieth century, as denoted by metrics such as the triple bottom line of economic, environmental, and equity goals (Elkington, 1999).

In this archetype, the logics of scientific analysis gain traction as there is a degree of acceptance of Anthropocene issues. Trajectories of some PBs, such as climate change and ozone depletion, may be slowed, or even reversed, to the extent that efforts to address them maintain the dominant logics of economic growth and corporate competitiveness. The term "rules" in this archetype is a double-entendre, referring both to the rules of the market logic as aided by the government, communities, and other spheres as well as the extent to which the market rules or dominates all aspects of life (both human and nonhuman). As Paul Hawkins, one proponent of this archetype, puts it:

> To create an enduring society, we will need a system of commerce and production where each and every act is inherently sustainable and restorative. Business will need to integrate, economic, biologic, and human systems

to create a sustainable method of commerce. As hard as we may try to become sustainable on a company-by-company level, we cannot fully succeed until the institutions surrounding commerce are redesigned. (Hawkins, 1993: xiv)

In this archetype, we see different cultural forms of market operating principles, from Scandinavian to Chinese State to American (Soskice & Hall, 2001). These market-oriented logics, while still predominant where the Anthropocene's main dimensions are concerned, are tempered by and blended with other logics, especially with state-, community-, and/or family-based logics. This admixture gives rise to both regulative and normative processes that encourage for-profit organizations to use voluntary agreements and serve environmentally sensitive consumers on different time horizons and valuations (Arsenio & Delmas, 2015; Slawinski et al., 2017).

Multiple organizational fields themselves become very complex in this archetype and revolve around specific Anthropocene dimensions that impact business competitiveness, such as climate change, water availability, and species loss. Institutional actors that represent market and state voices on either the transnational or the regional levels will play an important role in coordinating information flows, decisions, and cross-national action. As such, impacted industries, such as energy, automotive, and agriculture have disproportionate influence and power within PB fields that impact their interests. They may draw in NGOs, community groups, and social movements to create a set of field-level actors that include noncorporate actors to set the domain where many of the problems and solutions are identified and matched (Hoffman & Bertels, 2010), but the resultant field will always strive to frame issues as market based, requiring corporate actors to address them.

In this archetype, the state itself is a supporting actor for the market (i.e., corporate elites). Though it is not captured completely (as in Collapsed Systems), it negotiates outcomes with market stakeholders from different domains, depending on the specific field or logic. For instance, in the case of DDT regulation, the state played a co-equal role in helping frame conversations, direct hearings, and finally enacting guidelines and bans (Maguire & Hardy, 2009). In the current growth in renewable energy in China, the state is playing an even stronger role in promoting the emergent market both nationally and internationally (*Economist*, 2017b). Given the state's role, political change agents become more powerful champions of change. US President Obama was able to reshape the conversation around climate change, even though Congress was not a willing partner, by emphasizing the growing market in renewables. President Trump has similarly sought to undo those efforts, favoring the interests of incumbent energy sectors over new entrants. Interestingly, large players with positions in oil and natural gas (including fracking) and those with interest in renewables are able to agree more with gradual reduction of coal's role in the US energy economy as a means to maintain the dominance and legitimacy of the capitalist market and their particular sectors.

Events within Market Rules are framed as either standard weather events if solutions involve any form of restraint on the market, or cultural anomalies in the form of business opportunities if markets exist for solving them. Given that many skeptic countermovements hold a strong faith in the free market and the individual freedom to pursue business interests, their power within the field is muted by this framing. As long as efforts to address Anthropocene issues increase economic growth or create jobs, a counterargument to question the science of those issues gains little traction. Good business cases for key technologies, such as renewable energies, alternative drivetrains, or even nuclear power, will overcome attempts to deny the science and thereby deny the market opportunities. But any issue responses that may have negative impacts on the underlying logics of the market will be attacked by skeptic countermovements and minimized in their status and importance. As such, many Anthropocene issues will remain unaddressed, as there is no market opportunity around which to frame them.

5.3 The Technology Fix Archetype

In this archetype of Anthropocene Society, there is a belief that technology, if properly guided, will solve many environmental problems. As in the last archetype, the logics of scientific analysis gain some traction as there is a degree of acceptance of Anthropocene issues. Similarly, trajectories of some PB values, as measured by science-based outcome indicators (i.e., atmospheric GHG concentrations), would be lowered beneath threshold levels into safe zones. One example is the restoration of the ozone layer between 1990 and 2017 through recognition of the role of CFCs from various aerosol sources as the problem (Handwerk, 2010) and the negotiated agreement among business and government elites of the Montreal Protocol based on the successful pursuit of alternative technologies (i.e., HCFCs). The success of this effort in reversing one of the nine PBs has encouraged large groups of scientists, social observers and lay people to believe that further technological development in the area of "geo-engineering" (Crutzen, 2002; Steffen, Crutzen, & McNeil, 2007) might be an avenue for dealing with our current Anthropocene problems (but see Clark, 2014).

As part of this archetype, these groups generally agree that some forms of congruent governance is needed to develop and apply such large-scale scientific solutions (Galaz et al., 2012; Steffen et al., 2011). In other words, some form of Human Environment Systems (HES) design is needed and should be modeled and adjusted using complexity theory (Seidl et al., 2013).

> [E]xperimentation and deployment of all other geo-engineering technologies are likely to affect both local and regional scale ecosystems; systems that more often than not are being governed by natural resource users through local institutions, community management schemes, or transboundary part-nerships such as those that underpin marine spatial planning. (Galaz et al., 2012: 26)

The underlying logic of this archetype is based on the logics of professions, particularly around science and technology (Thornton et al., 2012). These logics are based on the notion that truth exists, and it can be discovered and verified through the scientific method, as applied by those rigorously trained (and vetted) in this method. This truth, itself, is a function of theoretical understanding and empirical abilities in a given period, and hence is modified as knowledge accumulates. Again, this modification is based on informed judgment made by groups of scientific peers that dominate the organizational field, where the role of engineers and informed policymakers tied to the domain of scientific exploration – "technologists" – is to translate these truths into workable technological solutions and delete those that limit the implementation of such solutions.

In this sense, the state as a logic has a role in the Technology Fix archetype, though subordinated to that of science as a profession (the collective of scientists, engineers, technicians, and informed policy analysts). There is also an implicit or explicit inclusion of the market and community as logics in the operation of the HES and governance systems, but always subordinated to the possibilities of technology. The values of the status quo underlying this arche-type, therefore, are guided by a preference for the preservation of the lifestyles found in advanced economies that created the Anthropocene problem in the first place (Anderson & Peters, 2016; Clark, 2014). Technology's ultimate focus is that of reducing our technological impact on the environment, but not necessarily changing the institutional values or beliefs that guide our actions.

It follows consistently in this archetype then that the key institutions are national and international scientific bodies and closely related science policy arms. In the case of climate change, the Paris Agreement working group (UNFCCC, 2017) might be elevated to a permanent regulatory agency with enforcement powers. In the case of biodiversity, new international bodies would be developed to rationalize current approaches to biodiversity and land use, and, as in the case of climate change, have enforcement powers, such as penalties, fines, tariffs, and budgets to help hire local antipoaching police.

The organizational fields themselves would become more vertically structured (Warren, 1967) and arranged around science- and engineering-focused bodies and policy groups (Jennings et al., 2011). Many markets and industries would continue to be organized around transactional versions of exchange, but their exchange would be mediated by how parties engage with the technical Anthropocene issues and system values. Power companies, for example, would collect information on carbon production and consumption that would be exchanged with scientific bodies for further improving community use of cleaner power. In the short run, these firms would be required to have a mix of renewables, remediation plans, and efficiency programs embedded in rates. In the long run, they would assess, track, and amend carbon output from the entire energy system, from generation through transmission, distribution, and use.

Entrepreneurs in this archetype would be those that provide technological solutions, so long as these solutions align with the fundamental technologist logic of the system. For instance, large-scale construction, manufacturing, and design firms would develop knowledge and technical capacities to carry out geo-engineering projects. The unintended technology failures and accidents (Perrow, 1999), such as those related to ozone depletion, nuclear power, or synthetic pesticides, would give rise to new sets of entrepreneurs that specialize in technology fixes and failures (Maguire & Hardy, 2009). Similarly, social movements would arise around new scientific truths and technology fixes, such as those now emerging to support and oppose GMO foods, nuclear power, vaccines, and wind farms (Davis et al., 2005; Hiatt & Park, 2013). Finally, regulatory change agents would take their cues from science institutes, agencies, entrepreneurs, and science-based social movements in the field, championing new policy through interdisciplinary, science-based working committees and rule-making groups in government.

Skeptic countermovements will hold stronger power in this archetype than the last if proposed Anthropocene solutions hold technological promise that is not accompanied by economic opportunity. This power will be even more pronounced if the state develops regulations that favor such technological development and that results in the diminishment of particular economic actors (i.e., "the government picking winners and losers in the market"). But, if technological advances lead to the development of new markets (such as electric cars), the diminishment of their power will mirror that in Market Rules.

Similar to Market Rules, events within Technology Fix will be framed as either standard weather events if technological solutions are not available, or cultural anomalies if technologies exist or can be developed for solving them. Any issues that have negative impact on the underlying logics of technology will be minimized in their status and importance. As such, many Anthropocene issues will remain unaddressed if there is no technological opportunity around which to frame them.

5.4 Conclusion

These three archetypes present a range of futures for humanity's response to the Anthropocene challenge that are held by constituents in organizational fields. The degree to which they are promoted and acted on – or used to block others' concerns – varies, as we have discussed in Section 3. Yet, each of them would seem to fall short in its own way of addressing the grand challenge of the Anthropocene. In the next section we will delve into a fourth archetype that represents an outline of what a fully engaged Anthropocene Society might look like.

6 A Fourth Archetype of Anthropocene Society: Cultural Re-Enlightenment

Though less consistently and coherently held as possible by analysts (Hamilton, 2014, 2015), there is a future for Anthropocene Society that might embrace forms of change on a scale necessary to ameliorate human impact on global ecosystems. Indeed, many experiments are presently under-way to create this emergent reality, some on the local level, like Kairos Earth in Vermont or the Monteverde Institute in Costa Rica, and others on the broader level, such as Sustainable Cities. Common to these experiments is a belief that we need to first shift our fundamental culture, values and behavior if we are going to make progress as a society in dealing with our negative effects on the Anthropocene. In the text that follows, we synthesize some of these points into the Cultural Re-Enlightenment archetype. At its root, this archetype is built on a recognition that "The [environmental] crisis is not simply something we can examine and resolve. We *are* the environmental crisis" (Evernden, 1985: 128). Put another way,

> The Anthropocene is not a problem for which there can be a solution. Rather, it names an emergent set of geo-social conditions that already fundamentally structure the horizon of human existence. It is thus not a new factor that can be accommodated within existing conceptual frameworks, including those within which policy is developed, but signals a profound shift in the human

relation to the planet that questions the very foundations of these frameworks themselves. (Rowan, 2014: 9)

This archetype would involve a cultural and institutional transition akin to the Enlightenment of the seventeenth and eighteenth centuries (Hoffman & Jennings, 2011) – hence the name "Re-Enlightenment." Where the first Enlightenment was built on a shift from perceiving nature as subsuming the human endeavor to one in which humankind embarked on the "conquest of nature" and a metaphor of the planet as an enemy to be subdued (Mirzoeff, 2014), this second Re-Enlightenment will reconnect natural and human systems into a cohesive cultural whole. The exact form of this variant of Anthropocene Society is more winding, its directions are more difficult to anticipate, and its timescale is much longer than the other three archetypes. But these other archetypes could be precursors to the Re-Enlightenment archetype discussed here. In many ways, this archetype can be presented only in aspirational terms. In the remainder of this section, we offer three elements of such an aspiration and then conclude with some broad discussion of the institutional elements around which it might be built.

6.1 The Limitations of the Contemporary Logics of Sustainable Development

Cultural Re-Enlightenment comes only with a reorientation of our way of thinking, invoking a different set of characters, seeking a different set of outcomes, and utilizing a different way of viewing ourselves and the world around us. It goes beyond the Brundtland Commission's definition of sustainable development as "development that meets the needs of the present without compromising the ability of future generations to meet their own needs" (World Commission on Environment and Development, 1987). This definition establishes a moral logic for addressing the boundaries of the Anthropocene – such as climate change, fisheries destruction, and habitat destruction – but is built upon the historic logics of economic and technological development that preside over the Collapsed Systems, Market Rules and Technology Fix archetypes. It simply, but more efficiently, maintains the status quo while seeking to include considerations for equity and the need for the affluent nations of the world to act; first, to ease poverty and the unfair burden that many of the world's poor bear in the face of our Anthropocene challenges, and second, to recognize the finite capacity of Earth to support all who are living today and all those who will inhabit the planet in the future. Most simply stated, it supports a logic that all have a right to have their needs met and strive for a lifestyle and consumptive patterns similar to an affluent westerner (Ehrenfeld & Hoffman, 2013).

As such, the overwhelming logic for the affluent nations to adhere to the Brundtland definition is consistent with historic market logics to maintain (or sustain) the standard of living that they have always enjoyed (Ehrenfeld, 2009). In the end, it is fundamentally built on and promotes an efficiency-based approach to improving existing systems and logics with minimal change. Though important for incremental change, this type of approach will not yield an ultimately positive Anthropocene Society as it rests on the same economics- and technological-based logics that created the meta-problem of the Anthropocene in the first place. In short, rather than creating sustainability it is about reducing unsustainability (Ehrenfeld, 2009). As such, it will slow the velocity of system decline but not reverse course. It has therefore become a set of institutions that has become diffused and deflected, becoming more jargon describing attempts to follow the same rules, but more efficiently and, to a lesser degree, more equitably. Instead, Cultural Re-Enlightenment must represent a departure from these historic notions of describing what we desire for a common and sustainable future that rests on a healthy planet.

6.2 The Logic of Sustainability-as-Flourishing

One way to reframe our institutional logics within Cultural Re-Enlightenment is around the concept of "sustainability-as-flourishing" as provided by Ehrenfeld (2009). This reconfiguration has two components.

The first component is the word "flourishing" and its connection to "the possibility that humans and other life will flourish on Earth forever" (Ehrenfeld, 2009). Flourishing means far more than to "sustain." It means to grow well, to prosper, to thrive, to live to the fullest. And, it pertains to allowing both human and natural systems to strive for a context in which all life can flourish.

> Flourishing is a dynamic word, representing change and striving, not the static sentiment that is projected by the word 'sustainable.' It is not a fixed end-state to be achieved, but a constant reaching for what it truly means to be living in an interconnected and complex world. It is a desirable future; one built not just on technological and material development, but also on cultural, psychological, and spiritual growth. (Ehrenfeld & Hoffman, 2013)

The second component refers to its compound nature. The word sustainability, by itself, refers to nothing in particular. It gathers meaning in a practical sense only when it is connected to the end being sought. For example, one could talk of sustainable growth, sustainable profits, or sustainable revenues. Ehrenfeld (2009) refers to "sustainability-as-flourishing" as a means to emphasize the quality of the goal being pursued, namely flourishing. In this way, sustainability-as-flourishing moves beyond standard environmental discourse around the problems to be solved and moves toward the need to nurture the possibility of a positive vision of the future. Ehrenfeld sees it being built at both the individual and systems levels.

At the level of the individual, sustainability-as-flourishing shifts our institutional logics from defining ourselves around the materials we possess to defining ourselves around the extent to which we act authentically. The first is about "having" and attending to our "needs"; the second is about "being" (Fromm, 1976) and attending to our "cares" (Ehrenfeld & Hoffman, 2013). The logics of flourishing then are focused on the realization of a sense of completeness, independent of our immediate material context. It challenges the dominant logics of Cartesian rationalism where the mind is separate from the body in engaging with the natural world. Instead, it is a challenge to see the world in authentic, intimate, and personal terms, and not just through the logics of modern culture.

At the level of the system, humans develop a clear understanding of their place within a complex systemic world, not as separate (and superior) to it but as part of it. With that recognition comes a structure of institutions that guide our responsibilities and bounds our action. Understanding this complexity demands a different set of institutions and logics about reality than found in the current objective view of the world where we discover reality only through scientific investigations and extend it through theorizing.

In the Cultural Re-Enlightenment archetype, the logics of scientific analysis are elevated and accepted but with bounds that are not present in the Market Rules or Technology Fix archetypes. It is tempered by a cautious approach to the overly rationalistic, technocratic thinking of the scientific method, with its preference for quantitative over qualitative measures and belief in a reductive focus on parts instead of the whole. At its most extreme, it is a rejection of "scientism," where truth becomes manifest *only* in the findings of the scientific method, explaining reality only by proving hypotheses through experiments. Stated in the simplest terms, this archetype challenges the dominant logics from which scientific truth views the world as a vast machine governed by analytically describable relationships that we can come to know only through objective science and that lead to institutions and technologies that we believe will always move the world in a progressive direction. In the same way, this kind of reductionist scientific reasoning treats the human being as a mechanistic organism that captures the real world in our minds through knowledge and operates on that knowledge according to some sort of logical calculus.

These rationally derived truths have become "social facts" (Durkheim, 1982) the taken-for-granted beliefs that guide our everyday life and that we teach to others as the correct way to think. Though this kind of scientific logic has produced much "progress" compared to the state of well-being that existed at the time of the Enlightenment, much of that progress has been measured by sets of generally quantitative, disparate metrics that fail to capture the holistic qualities of life. By other measures, real human progress on a systems scale has been declining. We are now beginning to understand that the world is not the complicated machine that Descartes and other Enlightenment thinkers thought it was. We, and the world, are complex and behave in nonlinear and unpredictable ways.

But the logics of sustainability-as-flourishing challenge the logics of Cartesian thinking and "rationality" upon which contemporary society is built. It calls for a move away from pure Enlightenment thinking where we are treated as separate from the world, where the evolution of "truths" that form human behavior and consciousness is divided between an external, ahistorical reality and the mind, which through its rational powers, recreates that external world inside our models of reality.

Cultural Re-Enlightenment embodies a set of logics that are emergent from the workings of the entire system, cannot be described by any reductionist set of rules and can be fully realized only through the multiple logics that reside within it; religion, philosophy, the humanities, the arts, the natural sciences as well as vernacular, pragmatic and indigenous experience. The logics of this archetype do not rule out the findings of scientific truths about the world that can be used to design and govern it, but they recognize that the scientific method alone cannot generate all of the knowledge needed to flourish in Anthropocene Society. Moving beyond a purely mechanical view of the social and natural worlds, this archetype would focus on the culture of which we are a part and the natural systems in which it is embedded. As such, the logics of science in Cultural Re-Enlightenment will be balanced by new logics of the state, market, community, religion, philosophy, and others, ones that are congruent with one another.

This balancing leads to an acknowledgment that the logics of sustainability-as-flourishing require new logics to replace the historic logics of the market which have perpetuated the dominant notion of the purpose of life as being materially driven, the nature of human interactions as being primarily transactional, the reality of the environment as an unlimited source of material resources and sink for wastes, and the possibility of unlimited economic and material growth. The economic and agentic logics that underlie our market logics assume that individuals strive to maximize desires, utilities, preferences, or some other measure of the priority of satisfaction. In the end, these logics distill utility down to money or material goods because that is easiest metric to measure and quantify. But it is this unquestioned and unbridled pursuit of money and material goods that is at the root of the Anthropocene crisis we now face.

The logics of the Cultural Re-Enlightenment archetype will move beyond the purely objective, quantitative, and "rational" logics of the material world to consider the spiritual, experiential, and pragmatic logics of the immaterial world. They will create a set of institutions that guide the world to stop consuming in the way that we do today. Though consumption is an inevitable consequence of life and of cultural existence for humans, there will be a shift in the way we consume, moving to a low- or no-growth economy as well as a carbon-neutral or carbon-negative society.

This shift will threaten specific institutions and actors within field-level debates. Reshaping the economic, political, and social structures will produce winners and losers. Those who possess power and benefit from the status quo in today's institutional reality, including politicians and corporate elites, will oppose any such move. As such, a radical reconfiguration of the organizational field will become necessary, correcting the underlying logics that drive our patterns of consumption (Ehrenfeld & Hoffman, 2013), which are based on extrinsic values that push us to consume to support our images in a culture in which material signs project who we are (Kasser, 2002) and an unceasing desire for novelty that maintains the continual desire for consumption as we upgrade our possessions to remain in sync with the expectations of a consumerist culture (Schor, 2010). Sustainability-as-flourishing changes our notions of consumption and their tight connection to personal fulfillment and satisfaction. Ultimately, they recognize our shared global responsibility for sharing the resources of Earth we all inhabit and diminishing the ways in which the entire system is depleting it.

6.3 Transcendence

In the logic of sustainability-as-flourishing, we recognize the logics of spirituality, philosophy and values, through which we experience connectedness to the web of life, illuminating our ties with other individuals, with the human community, and with nature. To counter Weber's sentiment, "The fate of our age, with its characteristic realization and intellectualization and above all the disenchantment of the world, is that the ultimate, most sublime values have withdrawn from public life" (Lassman, Velody, & Martins, 2015: 30), sustainability-as-flourishing recovers the sense of the complexity and sacredness of the world that envelops us. This process of recovery will diffuse from the dominant logics of science to the multiple everyday logics of society, helping us to live not just through the market logics of modern society but to develop new logics around environmental protection and connectedness as experienced through subjective engagement with the world in which we live, one in which we are relationally bound.

Through such a transition, we will recognize, in a deep and profound way, that the narcissistic needs that are directed inwardly are not as powerful or as enriching as the care that is directed outwardly toward other people (the social world) and nature (the natural world). In Cultural Re-Enlightenment, we will know the complex world and our place within it by adopting a new and more nuanced way of relating to it: blending objective elements of the scientific method with subjective elements of pragmatic, philosophical, and spiritual experience. Only when this fourth archetype takes on this deep form of meaning around us in terms of who we are as human, what is the environment that surrounds us, and what the connections between the two, can we begin to create the moral responsibilities to accept a stewardship role to replace our present materialist and exploitive role that we now embrace.

6.4 Institutional Elements of Cultural Re-Enlightenment

The institutions and logics around which the Cultural Re-Enlightenment archetype might be built will be marked by new institutions and social arrangements for coordination (Galaz et al., 2012; Johnson & Morehouse, 2014), predicated on the idea that the market and technology are merely the proximate cause of our dominating influence on the environment. Ultimately it will involve a change to our social beliefs and values that define their purpose, role, form, and impact (Bazerman & Hoffman, 1999). As such, the organizational field will include a constellation of actors who are more varied, diverse, and vertically structured than in the other archetypes. There would be a hierarchical arrangement among organizational groups, with science education, ethical action, religion, and community responsibility organizations at the apex (Karlsson, 2013) and economic growth or technocratic engineering being directed by their focus. Skeptical countermovements will be greatly muted as Anthropocene science becomes broadly accepted as a social fact (Durkheim, 1982).

Without a potent skeptic counterculture, Anthropocene events within the Cultural Re-Enlightenment archetype will be viewed and interpreted as cultural anomalies that will compel action to amend taken for granted assumptions about the human relation to nature (Hoffman & Jennings, 2011). Events such as hurricanes, the breakup of ice sheets, the opening of the Northwest Passage, or California's multiyear drought will emphasize broad-scale systems failures and will compel the mobilization of resources and action over meaning construction and solution development. In the development of those solutions, the main entrepreneurs will be more localized with social experiments emerging to find new ways of thinking and living that challenge outmoded and historic ways of knowing the world around us. These entrepreneurs would be focused on behavioral education, value appeals, and regional policy implementation along with the more traditional responses of technology and market development.

6.5 Conclusion

In the end, the Cultural Re-Enlightenment archetype is the more utopian of our four archetypes, representing a convergence among institutional fields and logics that both accept the reality of the Anthropocene and change our conceptions of what it means to be human, how the natural environment is understood and, most importantly, how the relationship between the two can be reconfigured.

7 Final Thoughts

It is now time to bring our Element to a close. We began with the question, "How might organization theory respond to the grand challenge represented by the Anthropocene Era?" We conclude with an encompassing answer that is dual in its form. First, we have also offered an amendment to organizational and institutional theory based on the challenges that the Anthropocene Era holds for the human race. Second, we offered four archetypes that are informed by those theories to imagine what our future Anthropocene Society might look like.

In retrospect, some form of duality can be the only acceptable answer. As the challenge of the Anthropocene represents a fundamentally new, and potentially devastating, emergent reality for humankind and the world we inhabit, the existing organizational theories that are strictly social in their scope are expected to be inadequate for the challenge at hand. A fully capable theory must realize the reconnection of *Naturewissenshaften* with *Kulturewissenshaften* that was proposed by Weber (1949) decades ago. The Anthropocene represents a world in which our impact on the environment is no longer external and separate. We can now vividly see that we are part of the environment because of the unprecedented ways in which we are an animating force in how it operates. This is unprecedented in the history of the planet.

In coming to terms with this unprecedented moment in history, we hope to have contributed one small step in bringing our social science more in line with geophysical realities, and in the process, offered some sense of the ways in which society might adapt or even flourish within a world that is changing around (and because of) us. While many critics of institutional theory hold that it is indifferent or agnostic to the political and environmental contexts which it studies, we are decidedly clear in our preference for the desired future that our institutional-political variant model elucidates. Only through a cultural and institutional shift on the scale of the Enlightenment of the seventeenth and eighteenth centuries will human societies come to terms with the reality it is creating for itself. Only through the aspiration towards the institutions, logics, and fields of Cultural Re-Enlightenment can the damaging processes that began with the "Great Acceleration" and continue today be reversed. The intermediate archetypes of Market Rules and Technology Fix will only prolong the inevitable and destructive outcome of Collapsing Systems. At this point in time, we can only hope that we are able to course correct and avoid the more dystopian alternatives.

Glossary

350.org A nonprofit organization that encourages action on the part of citizens and governments to reduce levels of carbon dioxide below 350 parts per million.

Aerosol loading (Planetary boundary - PB) Pollution and land-use changes that increases the release of dust and smoke. Aerosols affect cloud formation, patterns of atmospheric circulation, and the level of solar radiation that is reflected or absorbed in the atmosphere (Stockholm Resilience Center, 2018).

The Anthropocene A shift in our physical reality that is marked as a new geological epoch that reflects the extent to which human activity has become a significant influence on the operation of environmental systems. This label is proceeding through the formal stages of consideration and ratification the International Union of Geological Sciences (IUGS), the professional organization in charge of defining Earth's time scale.

Anthropocene Society A shift in our social reality that reflects the physical, institutional, and cultural changes that emerge within the Anthropocene Era. We are currently in Anthropocene Society.

AOSIS Alliance of Small Island States

ASEAN Association of Southeast Asian Nations

B Corporations Benefit Corporations

Biochemical flows (PB) The biogeochemical cycles of nitrogen and phosphorus have been radically changed by humans as a result of many industrial and agricultural processes, most notably fertilizer production and application. A significant fraction of the applied nitrogen and phosphorus makes its way to the sea, and can push marine and aquatic systems across ecological thresholds of their own (Stockholm Resilience Center, 2018).

Biosphere loss (PB) Loss of plant and animal species due to human activities have been more rapid in the past fifty years than at any time in human history, increasing the risks of abrupt and irreversible changes to ecosystems (Stockholm Resilience Center, 2018).

CFC Chlorofluorocarbon.

Climate change (PB) Concentrations of carbon dioxide in the atmosphere have risen from 280 ppm in preindustrial times to 400 ppm in 2014 – the widely recognized ceiling with regards to acceptable climate risk.

The world has already started to see the consequences with accelerated melting of the Greenland and West Antarctic ice sheets, sea level rise, and an increase in mortality in coral reefs (Stockholm Resilience Center, 2018).

COP 21   UN Conference of the Parties.

DDT   Dichlorodiphenyltrichloroethane. An often used chemical for eradicating mosquitoes and other pests, but one that accumulates in animals causing harmful effects.

ENGO   Environmental nongovernmental organization.

EPA   Environmental Protection Agency.

EU   European Union.

Freshwater use (PB)   Water is becoming increasingly scarce – by 2050 about half a billion people are likely to be subject to water stress, increasing the pressure to intervene in water systems (Stockholm Resilience Center, 2018).

GHG   Greenhouse gas.

GMO   Genetically Modified Organism.

HES   Human Environment Systems.

IEA   International Energy Agency.

Institution   Regulative, normative, and cultural-cognitive systems that provide meaning and descriptions of reality for organizations.

Institutional actor   The socially constructed entities engaged with the institutions of an organizational field.

Institutional logic   Sets of beliefs and practices that are deeply held and taken for granted as legitimate explanations of what is and what is not, what can be acted on and what cannot.

IPCC   Intergovernmental Panel on Climate Change.

Land-system change (PB)   Land that is converted to human use is one driving force behind the serious reductions in biodiversity, and it has impacts on water flows and on the biogeochemical cycling of carbon, nitrogen, and phosphorus and other important elements (Stockholm Resilience Center, 2018).

MNC   Multinational Corporation.

NGO   Nongovernmental organization.

Novel entities (PB)   Novel entities created entirely by humans includes the emissions of toxic compounds such as synthetic organic pollutants and radioactive materials, but also genetically modified organisms, nanomaterials, and micro-plastics. These can persist in the environment for a very long time, and their effects are potentially irreversible (Stockholm Resilience Center, 2018).

Ocean acidification (PB)   Around a quarter of the carbon dioxide humanity emits is ultimately dissolved in the oceans where it forms carbonic acid, decreasing the pH of the surface water and reducing the amount of available carbonate ions, an essential "building block" used by, e.g., corals, shellfish, and many plankton species to grow and survive. Compared to preindustrial times, surface ocean acidity has increased by 30 percent (Stockholm Resilience Center, 2018).

Organizational field   Relational spaces where multiple and often competing interests engage with other actors, often organized in communities, who may hold divergent ideas about the issues being contested.

Ozone depletion (PB)   The ozone layer in the atmosphere filters out harmful ultraviolet (UV) radiation from the sun. In the 1980s increased concentration of ozone-depleting chemical substances resulted in a thinning of this protective layer, called the Antarctic ozone "hole." Because of the actions taken as a result of the Montreal Protocol, we appear to be on a path that will allow us to stay within this boundary (Stockholm Resilience Center, 2018).

Paris Agreement   A 2015 agreement among 196 countries within the United Nations Framework Convention on Climate Change dealing with greenhouse gas emissions mitigation, adaptation, and finance starting in the year 2020.

PB   Planetary Boundaries. Nine "thresholds below which humanity can safely operate and beyond which the stability of planetary-scale systems cannot be relied upon" (Gillings & Hagan-Lawson, 2014).

PPM   Parts per million.

SAF   Strategic Action Field.

TVA   Tennessee Valley Authority.

UNFCCC   United Nations Framework Convention on Climate Change.

WWF   World Wildlife Fund.

Appendix
Modifying Institutional Research Methods to Engage with the Anthropocene

As a postscript for our readers, many of whom may have graduate degrees and an interest in research, we briefly discuss three implications for examining the operation of organizations in the Anthropocene Era: modifying data collection; modifying methods of analysis and; linking qualitative with quantitative methods.

A.1 Modifying Data Collection

The scientific data from the Anthropocene are large scale, multimodal, and temporal. As discussed in Section 1, the "Great Acceleration" model is based on several patterns of exponential acceleration, from population growth and economic development to urbanization and health, which have occurred since the Industrial Revolution and more noticeably since World War II. Such data are readily available through agencies such as the United Nations, UNESCO, the World Bank, and the International Energy Agency. Data on PBs are kept by some of these institutions, notably the IPCC and the Stockholm Resilience Center. The "Ecosystems Breakdowns" model is based on these PB thresholds being crossed and increasing evidence of collapse events and cascades, such as in the rapid disappearance of bees in many regions. Many scientific studies exist of each, and some have been compiled in holistic manuscripts, such as *Collapse* (Diamond, 2005) or *The Sixth Extinction* (Kolbert, 2014).

Social science research and the forms of data collected would need to be integrated with these types of scientific data. Consequently, we would need to see some efforts to parallel or match the large-scale, multimodal, longitudinal data efforts in different physical science domains. We offer five more specific modifications in the paragraphs that follow.

The first modification would be increasing the time scale of our studies, with the window more on the order of 20 to 50 years. The shorter times (5 to 10 years) that are standard in the social sciences are useful for panel analyses, because they offer sufficient temporal and unit variance for general linear models (Beck & Katz, 1995). But the 20- to 50-year window allows for more temporal and unit variation within particular groups of variables, as well as the incorporation of more system shifts, trends, and lag effects (Greene, 2003). These data would also match up better with science-based acceleration data, such as GHG rises, storms, and drought patterns. Political economists, such as Piketty (2014) and Ferguson (2008) have led the way in this regard, being willing to study one or two centuries' worth of data on market rises, social inequality, and financing. In sociology, Meyer, Boli, Thomas and Ramirez (1999) have led the way with such studies of the World Polity. Research into environmental treaties and assessments have followed the same exponential diffusion curve that we see with many of the great accelerations (Frank, Hironaka, & Schofer, 2000).

The second modification would be using "big data" to capture these long tails, and multilevel phenomena. Fortunately, we are in an era of big data (Kitchin & McArdle, 2016), and accessing and assembling such information is becoming easier. Many international agencies, such as the International Energy Agency and the World Intellectual Property Organization, collect long-term, systematic data on economies and societies, not just on natural phenomena. Google has also launched efforts at capturing longitudinal, multimodal data that is shared from Google Cloud Data (i.e., Earth Engine) or designed by Google Analytics (for a fee). There are also Web scrapers, such as Cultr, which can be used to gather multimodal data for ENGO and activist web sites. These data are both about the science of the Anthropocene and social efforts work with such data.

A third modification, which is partly an alternative to these multimodal data with long tails, would be to launch more studies of threshold events. All three models of the Anthropocene Era rely upon such events, so modifying data collection to collect events, crises, and tipping points would appear to be the new rigueur-du-jour. Crises, such as Fukushima or Hurricane Katrina, which have already been examined by social scientists (i.e., Aoki & Rothwell, 2013; Hackler, 2011), might be studied as individual cases using interviews, on-site observation, and archival information, just as has been done with the Deepwater Horizon disaster (Harvey, 2016; Hoffman & Jennings, 2015).

One characteristic that might distinguish these event studies from past efforts would be the effort to contextualize them as part of the larger problem of the Anthropocene. For instance, the Schussler, Ruling, and Wittneben (2014) study of COP 21 clearly situates itself in the twenty-year history of prior climate change meetings and growing need to deal with climate change (also see Maguire & Hardy, 2009 on DDT). In addition, choosing potential or actual field configuring events or cultural anomalies (Hoffman & Jennings, 2015; Hoffman & Ocasio, 2001) would help to examine extreme cases of institutional processes (Eisenhardt & Graebner, 2007). Hurricane Katrina may be one such defining event (Harvey, 2016), while Hurricane Irma – in spite of its terrible damage – may be less impactful due to the total property damage value. Hurricanes Sandy and Harvey, which were less cataclysmic in geophysical terms, still have higher total estimated damages in actual and nominal dollars

(Amadeo, 2017) and impacted more influential constituencies for creating change (Molotch, 1970).

A fourth modification, which is in the spirit of contextualizing data, would be to have such cases based on and immersed in complex physical and social science data about the Anthropocene event. In that way, the linkages with the various dimensions of the Anthropocene models and institutional domains of Anthropocene Society could be made richer and more robust. Because the narrow disciplinary focus of academic journals as well as journal article size and researcher capacity are not likely to change in the foreseeable future, this modification would be a challenge for successful publication. The scope of the event crisis would likely need to be narrowed in order to have sufficient space for traditional depth and added breadth. The meaning of a crisis (i.e., Deepwater Horizon), practice (i.e., use of DDT), or event (i.e., Conference of the Parties [COP] meeting) would be viewed from different levels in the institution (Greenwood et al., 2015) and rolled somewhat backward and forward to create a sensible whole (Reinecke & Ansari, 2017).

A fifth and final modification would be to rely more on data from natural or planned experiments. Given the need to match physical and social science data, it is likely that a physical science event would be viewed by social scientists before, during, and after the event. For example, how has risk and insurance worked before, during, and after Hurricane Katrina versus the Sandy–Harvey–Irma–Maria constellation might be compared and contrasted. Katrina might be viewed as one of the last non-Anthropocene (climate-change) perceived hurricanes, and this latest trio, as one of the first truly perceived Anthropocene group. If the latter grouping is really post-Holocene in conceptualization and discourse, the reaction of institutions such as insurers and local governments are likely to have changed fundamentally.

Data from planned interventions would likely be better scoped than the massive data from events such as droughts and hurricanes. But, like these other events, planned interventions would be gathered before, during and after the focal phenomena. Increasingly, we see policy effects studied in management and organization theory as treatment effects, though there has been a longer history of viewing them as such in economics. One can imagine that pro-renewable energy policies will increasingly examined (Hiatt & Park, 2013; Sine & Lee, 2009).

A.2 Modifying Methods of Analysis

An adage in methodology is that when a theory or a field is changing, more qualitative analysis is likely to be useful (Edmondson & McManus, 2007).

Therefore, the collection of more multimodal, longitudinal events and crisis-focused data would challenge the mainstream single longitudinal case analyses, which are often seen in qualitative research on organizations. As a start, there is a need for more contextual, horizontal, and longitudinal information to be employed in such studies. In light of this range and scale of data, it would be useful to have preprocessing and multiorganizing efforts at observation. One might use, for example, topic modeling (Grimmer & Stewart, 2013) as a way of sorting through data, finding new topics and creating new connections. Additionally, in this era of big data about the Anthropocene and the multilayers of institutions and processes, it is better not to assume too much about how institutional dynamics work. Instead, practices will be less directly observable and only known through constellations of topics such that their diffusion will be observed through constellations or secondary topics (DiMaggio, 2015). For instance, risk and insurance for hurricanes require data analytics that might diffuse gradually, changing how insurance is practiced.

Another likely adjustment to qualitative data analysis would be a reliance on even more advanced processual models. Anthropocene data, as discussed earlier, have longer time horizons – both looking forward and backward. Any systematic approach to finding meaning in such data would require a model that captures some of this long temporality (Reinecke & Ansari, 2017). This does not put a premium on historical case analysis per se, but it does imply that cross-sectional analysis using axial coding for orders of meaning will not be quite as useful as they have been in past institutional studies. What will be more interesting is developing convincing narrative about how new Anthropocene processes, such as the Paris Agreement or antipoaching rules, were created from or merged with older institutional structures.

A.3 Linking Qualitative and Quantitative Methods

Even with this need for more qualitative analysis to establish new social science from physical science phenomena, we anticipate a shift to attach them to quantitative analysis. The most obvious changes to qualitative models stem from fitting the data to the Anthropocene, which would include exponential curves with long tails and some very recent rapid shifts with narrow amplitude. As a general rule, nonlinear models for such curves, either in the form of increasing counts across categories (i.e., negative binomials) or threshold changes by groups (i.e., multinomials), would require multiple panels of data that would be adjusted using residual analysis and reweighted clustering (Greene, 2003).

However, event-focused models that attempt to capture something specific about the underlying nonstandard distribution of events and their timing would seem more fruitful to examine basic, disaggregated data and assume less about features and time-scaled behavior (Greve, 2017). It would be then useful to try some temporal event history or threshold models (Tuma & Hannan, 1984) such as, for example, environmental assessments, which have spread through regular diffusion patterns, though there are complexities in their actual enforcement levels (Schofer & Hironaka, 2005).

A strategy that would be consistent with the newer forms of data collected in the Anthropocene would be to focus on thresholds and events as independent variables. These events (either naturally occurring or generated by institutional actors) could be viewed as interventions or treatment effects. As a result, models accounting for lag and shock effects, such as of spills on the market or stakeholder support for action (Flammer, 2013), might use difference in differences models (changing slope and systems) (Aichele & Felbermayr, 2015).

A more fundamental way of adjusting the antecedents or causal aspects of these models is to collect the data based on actual, planned experiments, which is more common in the physical sciences than in institutional theory. This is due, in part, to the ability of laboratories to allow sufficient control over conditions and randomization of units to be treated and compared to the untreated (control) group. As a result, the treatment effects can be isolated and estimated accurately. Management studies has seen a rise in more qualitative pilot studies of issues like inclusion, followed by experimental studies (see Jones, Comfort, & Hillier, 2015; Li et al., 2014). The advantages of these experiments are clear; they are visible, clean, and easy to promulgate in repeated studies. They are also good at isolating vectors and key mechanisms. There is always, of course, the issue of scale (transferable or not) and whether the conditions themselves are overly controlled for true "field" work. So, it would seem useful to adopt the same mixed methodology in institutional work on the Anthropocene.

A final quantitative method of note for Anthropocene studies of institutional-political processes is simulation. Simulations are used in the natural sciences once science reaches the point of application, such as engineering systems studies (see Marshall & Brown, 2003; Polhill et al., 2016, for reviews). These models are based on well-defined constructs, often associated with readily observable entities, such as a plot of ground or amount of solar energy received in a domain, to which are added some new class of entity, a change in process, a feedback loop, some set of exogenous variables, and key values levels for variables that can be established and banded. The model is then run through multiple rounds with some version of randomization (i.e., Monte Carlo) and updating (Verstegen et al., 2016) in order to determine converging and stable parameter values. These models are increasingly used on a micro scale for scoping project success factors and on a macro scale, such as in climate change modeling.

Such environmental simulation models are not likely to be used for institutional-political systems or specific processes, but we believe that they are likely to be either attached to such social science analyses or become the focus of them. The outputs of these models still require translation into acceptable sociopolitical actions. The institutional-political models of transnational and regional policy negotiations are likely to rely on such models, as they did in the COP 21 and Paris Agreement meetings. So, understanding and bringing such data and the specific models more directly into institutional research would seem a next methodological step. Part of this step involves consideration of the construction and nature of these models. Questions such as how they are viewed in terms of "scientific truth," who promotes them, who resists them, and on what specific grounds they are resisted would be of great interest to institutional scholars. After all, Allison's famous Cuban Missile Crisis study (1971), which contains sections on how Soviet actions were modeled and portrayed by the bureaucracy and in the military, has become a classic of organization theory.

References

Aichele, R., & Felbermayr, G. (2015). Kyoto and carbon leakage: An empirical analysis of the carbon content of bilateral trade. *Review of Economics and Statistics*, 97(1), 104–115.

Allison, G. T. (1971). *Essence of Decision*. Boston, MA: Little, Brown.

Amadeo, K. (2017). How hurricanes damage the economy: Why Harvey, Irma, Maria and other hurricanes are so destructive. The Balance, Nov. 14. Retrieved from: https://www.thebalance.com/hurricane-damage-eco nomic-costs-4150369

Anderson, K., & Peters, G. (2016). The trouble with negative emissions. *Science*, 354, 182–183.

Ansari, S., Wijen, F., & Gray, B. (2013). Constructing a climate change logic: An institutional perspective on the 'tragedy of the commons.' *Organization Science*, 24(4), 1014–1040.

Aoki, M., & Rothwell, G. (2013). A comparative institutional analysis of the Fukushima nuclear disaster: Lessons and policy implications. *Energy Policy*, 53, 240–247.

Arsenio, O. I., & Delmas, M. (2015). Nonprice incentives and energy conservation. *Proceedings of the National Academy of Sciences of the USA*, 112(6), E510–E515.

Ball, J., Reicher, D., Sun, X., & Pollock, C. (2017). *The New Solar System: China's Evolving Solar Industry and Its Implications for Competitive Solar Power in the United States and the World*. Stanford, CA: Stanford University Press.

Bansal, P., & Hoffman, A. (eds.). (2012). *Oxford Handbook on Business and the Natural Environment*. Oxford: Oxford University Press.

Baron, J., Dobbin, F., & Jennings, P. D. (1986). War and peace: The evolution of modern personnel administration in US industry. *American Journal of Sociology*, 92(2), 350–383.

Bazerman, M., & Hoffman, A. (1999). Sources of environmentally destructive behavior: Individual, organizational and institutional perspectives. *Research in Organizational Behavior*, 21, 39–79.

Beck, N., & Katz, J. (1995). What to do (and not to do) with time-series cross-section data. *American Political Science Review*, 89, 634–647.

Benson, J. K. (1977). Organizations: A dialectical view. *Administrative Science Quarterly*, 22(1), 1–21.

Bertels, S., Hoffman, A., & DeJordy, R. (2014). The varied work of challenger movements: Identifying challenger roles in the U.S. environmental movement. *Organization Studies*, 35(8), 1171–1210.

Bevir, M. (1999). Foucault, M. power, and institutions. *Political Studies*, 47, 345–359.

Biermann, F., Abbott, K., Andersen, S., Bäckstrand, K., Bernstein, S., Betsill, M., & Gupta, A. (2012). Navigating the Anthropocene: Improving earth system governance. *Science*, 335(6074), 1306–1307.

Blee, K., & Creasap, K. (2010). Conservative and right-wing movements. *Annual Review of Sociology*, 36, 269–286.

Bourdieu, P. (1977). *Outline of a Theory of Practice*, Vol. 16. Cambridge: Cambridge University Press.

Bourdieu, P. (2011). The forms of capital. *Cultural Theory: An Anthology*, 1, 81–93.

Bourdieu, P., & Wacquant, L. (1992). *Invitation to Reflexive Sociology*. Chicago, IL: University of Chicago Press.

Brulle, R. (2014). Institutionalizing delay: Foundation funding and the creation of US climate change counter-movement organizations. *Climatic Change*, 122, 681–694.

Burrell, G., & Morgan, G. (1979). *Sociological Paradigms and Organizational Analysis*, Portsmouth, NH: Heinemann.

Castells, M. (2015). *Networks of Outrage and Hope: Social Movements in the Internet Age*. Hoboken, NJ: John Wiley & Sons.

Chandler, A. D. (1962). *Strategy and Structure: Chapters in the History of the American Enterprise*. Cambridge, MA: MIT Press.

Clark, N. (2014). Geo-politics and the disaster of the Anthropocene. *The Sociological Review*, 62(S1), 19–37.

Clear Path. (2015). *Republicans, Clean Energy and Climate Change*. Echelon Insights, North Star Opinion Research, and Public Opinion Strategies. Retrieved from: https://assets.clearpath.org/2016/09/clearpath_survey_re port.pdf

Clegg, S. (2010). The state, power, and agency: Missing in action in institutional theory? *Journal of Management Inquiry*, 19(1), 4–13.

Cobb, C., Halstead, T., & Rowe, J. (1995). *The Genuine Progress Indicator: Summary of Data and Methodology*, Vol. 15, San Francisco, CA: Redefining Progress.

Cohen, W. M., & Levinthal, D. A. (1990). Absorptive capacity: A new perspective on learning and innovation. *Administrative Science Quarterly*, 35(1), 128–152.

Colignon, R. (1997). *Power Plays: Critical Events in the Institutionalization of the Tennessee Valley Authority*. Albany, NY: SUNY Press.

Cooter, A. (2013). *Americanness, Masculinity, and Whiteness: How Michigan Militia Men Navigate Evolving Social Norms*, Ann Arbor, MI: University of Michigan.

Costello, A., et al. (2009). Managing the health effects of climate change. *The Lancet*, 373, 1693–1733.

Crutzen, P. (2002). Geology of mankind. *Nature*, 415, 23.

Crutzen, P., & Stoermer, E. (2000). The 'Anthropocene.' *Global Change Newsletter*, 41, 17–18.

Czarniawska, B., & Sevón, G. (eds.). (1996). *Translating Organizational Change*, Vol. 56. Berlin: Walter de Gruyter.

Dacin, M. T., Goodstein, J., & Scott, W. R. (2002). Institutional theory and institutional change: Introduction to the special research forum. *Academy of Management Journal*, 45(1), 45–56.

Davis, G. F., & Marquis, C. (2005). Prospects for organization theory in the early twenty-first century: Institutional fields and mechanisms. *Organization Science*, 16(4), 332–343.

Davis, G. F., Morrill, C., Rao, H., & Soule, S. A. (2008). Introduction: Social movements in organizations and markets. *Administrative Science Quarterly*, 53(3), 389–394.

Davis, G. F., & Zald, M. N. (2005). Social change, social theory, and the convergence of movements and organizations. In G. Davis, D. McAdam, W. R. Scott, & M. Zald (eds.), *Social Movements and Organization Theory*. New York, NY: Cambridge University Press, pp. 335–350.

De Villiers, M. (2001). *Water: The Fate of Our Most Precious Resource*. New York, NY: Houghton Mifflin Harcourt.

Diamond, J. (1999). *Guns, Germs and Steel: The Fates of Human Societies*. New York, NY: Norton & Company.

Diamond, J. (2005). *Collapse: How Societies Choose to Fail or Succeed*. New York, NY: Penguin Books.

DiMaggio, J. (1988). Interest and agency in institutional theory. In L. Zucker (ed.), *Institutional Patterns and Organizations*, Cambridge, MA: Ballinger, pp.3–21.

DiMaggio, P. (2015). Adapting computational text analysis to social science (and vice versa). *Big Data & Society*, 2(2), November, 1–5.

DiMaggio, P., & Powell, W. (1983). The iron cage revisited: Institutional isomorphism and collective rationality in organizational fields. *American Sociological Review* 48, 147–160.

Dobbin, F. (2009). *Inventing Equal Opportunity*. Princeton, NJ: Princeton University Press.

Douglas, M., & Wildavsky, A. (1982). *Risk and Culture: An Essay on the Selection of Technical and Environmental Dangers*. Berkeley, CA: University of California Press.

Dowd, T., Glynn, M., & Lounsbury, M. (2017). Advances in cultural entrepreneurship: Looking back and moving forward. *Academy of Management Proceedings*, 1, 14466.

Downs, A. (1967). *Inside Bureaucracy: A RAND Corporation Research Study*. Long Grove, IL: Waveland Press.

Downs, A. (1972). Up and down with ecology: The issue-attention cycle. *Public Interest*, 28 (Summer), 38–50.

Durand, R., & Paolella, L. (2013). Category stretching: Reorienting research on categories in strategy, entrepreneurship, and organization theory. *Journal of Management Studies*, 50(6), 1100–1123.

Durkheim, É. (1982). *The Rules of the Sociological Method*, S. Lukes, ed., W. Halls, translator. New York, NY: Free Press.

Economist. (2017a). Trump's indifference to climate change has not changed China's view. *The Economist*, April 20. Retrieved from: www.economist.com/china/2017/04/20/trumps-indifference-to-climate-change-has-not-changed-chinas-view

Economist. (2017b). A communist party gathering in China will test Xi Jinping's power. *The Economist*, September 7. Retrieved from: www.economist.com/china/2017/09/07/a-communist-party-gathering-in-china-will-test-xi-jinpings-power

Edmondson, A. C., & McManus, S. E. (2007). Methodological fit in management field research. *Academy of Management Review*, 32(4), 1246–1264.

Ehrenfeld, J. (2009). *Sustainability by Design: A Subversive Strategy for Transforming Our Consumer Culture*. New Haven, CT: Yale University Press.

Ehrenfeld, J., & Hoffman, A. (2013). *Flourishing: A Frank Conversation on Sustainability*, Palo Alto, CA: Stanford University Press.

Eisenhardt, K., & Graebner, M. (2007). Theory building from cases: Opportunities and challenges. *Academy of Management Journal*, 50(1), 25–32.

Elkington, J. (1999). *Cannibals with Forks: The Triple Bottom Line of 21st Century Business*. London: Capstone Publishing.

Espeland, W. N. (1998). *The Struggle for Water: Politics, Rationality, and Identity in the American Southwest*. Chicago, IL: University of Chicago Press.

Evernden, N. (1985). *The Natural Alien: Humankind and the Environment*. Toronto: University of Toronto Press.

Ferguson, N. (2008). *The Ascent of Money: A Financial History of the World.* New York, NY: Penguin Books.

Ferraro, F., Etzion, D., & Gehman, J. (2015). Tackling grand challenges pragmatically: Robust action revisited. *Organization Studies,* 36(3), 363–390.

Feygina, I., Jost, J., & Goldsmith, R. (2010). System justification, the denial of global warming and the possibility of 'system sanctioned change.' *Personality and Social Psychology Bulletin,* 36(3), 326–338.

Fiss, P., & Hirsch, P. (2005). The discourse of globalization: Framing and sensemaking of an emerging concept. *American Sociological Review,* 70, 29–52.

Flammer, C. (2013). Corporate social responsibility and shareholder reaction: The environmental awareness of investors. *Academy of Management Journal,* 56(3), 758–781.

Fligstein, N., & McAdam, D. (2011). Toward a general theory of strategic action fields. *Sociological Theory,* 29(1), 1–26.

Fligstein, N., & McAdam, D. (2012). *A Theory of Fields.* Oxford: Oxford University Press.

Foucault, M. (1977). *Discipline and Punishment.* New York, NY: Pantheon Books.

Foucault, M. (2007). *Security, Territory, Population: Lectures at the Collège de France, 1977–78.* New York, NY: Springer.

Frank, D., Hironaka, A., & Schofer, E. (2000). The nation-state and the natural environment over the twentieth century. *American Sociological Review,* 65, 96–116.

Friedland, R., & Alford, R. (1991). Bringing society back in: Symbols, practices and institutional contradictions. In P. DiMaggio & W. Powell (eds.), *The New Institutionalism in Organizational Analysis.* Chicago, IL: The University of Chicago Press, pp.232–263.

Fromm, E. (1976). *To Have or To Be?* New York, NY: Harper & Row.

Galaz, V., et al. (2012). 'Planetary boundaries': Exploring the challenges for global environmental governance. *Current Opinion in Environmental Sustainability,* 4, 80–87.

Garud, R., & Karnøe, P. (2003). Bricolage versus breakthrough: Distributed and embedded agency in technology entrepreneurship. *Research Policy,* 32(2), 277–300.

Gavetti, G., & Levinthal, D. (2000). Looking forward and looking backward: Cognitive and experiential search. *Administrative Science Quarterly,* 45(1), 113–137.

Gedajlovic, E., Cao, Q., & Zhang, H. (2012). Corporate shareholdings and organizational ambidexterity in high-tech SMEs: Evidence from a transitional economy. *Journal of Business Venturing,* 27(6), 652–665.

Gehman, J., Trevino, L., & Garud, R. (2013). Values work: A process study of the emergence and performance of organizational values practices. *Academy of Management Journal*, 56(1), 84–112.

Georg, S., & Hoffman, A. (eds.). (2013). *Business and the Natural Environment: Critical Perspectives on Business and Management*. London: Routledge.

Giddens, A. (1984). *The Construction of Society*. Cambridge: Polity Press.

Giddens, A. (2009). *The Politics of Climate Change*. Cambridge: Polity Press.

Gillings, M., & Hagan-Lawson, E. (2014). The cost of living in the Anthropocene. *Earth Perspectives*, 1, 2.

Giorgi, S., Lockwood, C., & Glynn, M. (2015). The many faces of culture: Making sense of 30 years of research on culture in organization studies. *The Academy of Management Annals*, 9(1), 1–54.

Goffman, E. (1974). *Frame Analysis: An Essay on the Organization of Experience*. Cambridge, MA: Harvard University Press.

Gordon, C. (ed.). (1980). *Power/Knowledge: Selected Interviews and Other Writings, 1972–1977, Michael Foucault*. New York, NY: Pantheon.

Gouldner, A. (1954). *Patterns of Industrial Bureaucracy*. New York, NY: Free Press.

Gramsci, A. (1995). *Further Selections from the Prison Notebooks*. Minneapolis, MN: University of Minnesota Press.

Gray, B., Purdy, J. M., & Ansari, S. S. (2015). From interactions to institutions: Microprocesses of framing and mechanisms for the structuring of institutional fields. *Academy of Management Review*, 40(1), 115–143.

Greene, W. (2003). *Econometric Analysis*. Delhi: Pearson Education, India.

Greenwood, R., & Hinings, C. R. (1993). Understanding strategic change: The contribution of archetypes. *Academy of Management Journal*, 36(5), 1052–1081.

Greenwood, R., Jennings, P. D., & Hinings, R. (2015). Sustainability and organizational change: An institutional perspective. In R. Henderson, R. Gulati, & M. Tushman (eds.), *Leading Sustainable Change: An Organizational Perspective*. Oxford: Oxford University Press, pp.323–355.

Greenwood, R., Oliver, C., Suddaby, R., & Sahlin-Andersson, K. (2008). *The SAGE Handbook of Organizational Institutionalism*. London: SAGE Publications.

Greenwood, R., Raynard, M., Kodeih, F., Micelotta, E. R., & Lounsbury, M. (2011). Institutional complexity and organizational responses. *Academy of Management Annals*, 5(1), 317–371.

Greve, H. (2017). *Data display for Administrative Science Quarterly*. Presentation at the Academy of Management, ASQ Board Meeting, Atlanta, GA.

Grimmer, J., & Stewart, B. M. (2013). Text as data: The promise and pitfalls of automatic content analysis methods for political texts. *Political Analysis*, 21(3), 267–297.

Hackler, M. (ed.). (2011). *Culture after the Hurricanes: Rhetoric and Reinvention on the Gulf Coast*. Jackson, MS: University Press of Mississippi.

Hamilton, C. (1999). The genuine progress indicator methodological developments and results from Australia. *Ecological Economics*, 30(1), 13–28.

Hamilton, C. (2014). The delusion of the 'good Anthropocene': Reply to Andrew Revkin. Retrieved from: http://clivehamilton.com/the-delusion-of-the-good-anthropocene-reply-to-andrew-revkin/

Hamilton, C. (2015). The theodicy of the "good Anthropocene." *Environmental Humanities*, 7, 233–238.

Handwerk, B. (2010). Whatever happened to ozone holes? *National Geographic*, May 7, 2010.

Hardy, C., & Maguire, S. (2008). Institutional entrepreneurship. In R. Greenwood, C. Oliver, T. Lawrence, & R. Meyer (eds.), *The SAGE Handbook of Organizational Institutionalism*. London: SAGE, pp.198–217.

Harvey, D. C. (2016). The discourse of the ecological Precariat: Making sense of social disruption in the Lower Ninth Ward in the long-term aftermath of Hurricane Katrina. *Sociological Forum*. 31 (S1), 862–884.

Harvey, D. (1990). *The Condition of Postmodernity: An Enquiry into the Conditions of Cultural Change*. Oxford: Blackwell.

Hawken, P. (1993). *Ecology of Commerce: How Business Can Save the Planet*. New York, NY: Harper Business.

Heath, Y., & Gifford, R. (2006). Free-market ideology and environmental degradation: The case of belief in global climate change. *Environment and Behavior*, 38(1), 48–71.

Hiatt, S., & Park, S. (2013). Lords of the harvest: Third-party influence and regulatory approval of genetically modified organisms. *Academy of Management Journal*, 56(4), 923–944.

Hirsch, P. M., & Lounsbury, M. (1997). Ending the family quarrel: Toward a reconciliation of "old" and "new" institutionalisms. *American Behavioral Scientist*, 40(4), 406–418.

Hoffman, A. (1999). Institutional evolution and change: Environmentalism and the US chemical industry. *Academy of Management Journal*, 42(4), 351–371.

Hoffman, A. (2011). Talking past each other? Cultural framing of skeptical and convinced logics in the climate change debate. *Organization & Environment*, 24 (1), 3–33.

Hoffman, A. (2015). *How Culture Shapes the Climate Change Debate.* Palo Alto, CA: Stanford University Press.

Hoffman, A. (2018). The next phase of business sustainability. *Stanford Social Innovation Review,* Spring: 34–39.

Hoffman, A., & Bertels, S. (2010). Who is part of the environmental movement? Assessing network linkages between NGOs and corporations. In T. Lyon (ed.), *Good Cop Bad Cop: Environmental NGOs and Their Strategies toward Business.* Washington, DC: Resources for the Future Press, pp.48–69.

Hoffman, A., & Jennings, P.D. (2011). The BP oil spill as a cultural anomaly? Institutional context, conflict and change. *Journal of Management Inquiry,* 20(2), 100–112.

Hoffman, A., & Jennings, P. D. (2015). Institutional theory and the natural environment: Research in (and on) the Anthropocene. *Organization & Environment,* 28(1), 8–31.

Hoffman, A., & Ocasio, W. (2001). Not all events are attended equally: Toward a middle-range theory of industry attention to external events. *Organization Science,* 12(4), 414–434.

Holt, R. (2006). Making a virtue out of a necessity: Hurricanes and the resilience of community organization. *Proceedings of the National Academy of Sciences of the USA,* 103(7), 2005–2006.

Hulme, M. (2009). *Why We Disagree About Climate Change: Understanding Controversy, Inaction and Opportunity.* Cambridge: Cambridge University Press.

Intergovernmental Panel on Climate Change (IPCC) (2017). Retrieved from: www.ipcc.ch/

Jasper, J. M. (2010). Cultural approaches in the sociology of social movements. In *Handbook of Social Movements across Disciplines.* New York, NY: Springer Science+Business Media, pp.59–109.

Jasper, J. M. (2014). *Nuclear Politics: Energy and the State in the United States, Sweden, and France.* Princeton, NJ: Princeton University Press.

Jennings, P. D., & Hoffman, A. (2017). Institutional theory and the natural environment: Building research through tensions and paradox. In R. Greenwood, C. Oliver, T. Lawrence, & R. Meyer (eds.), *The SAGE Handbook of Organizational Institutionalism,* 2nd edn. London: SAGE Publications, pp.759–785.

Jennings, P. D., Zandbergen, P., & Martins, M. (2011). An institutional view of process strategy in the public sector. In P. Mazzola & F. Kellermann (eds.), *Handbook of Strategy Process Research.* Cheltenham: Edward Elgar Publishing, pp.492–517.

Johnson, E., & Morehouse, H. (eds.). (2014) After the Anthropocene: Politics and geographic inquiry for a new epoch. *Progress in Human Geography*, 38(3), 439–456.

Jones, P., Comfort, D., & Hillier, D. (2015). Spotlight on solar farms. *Journal of Public Affairs*, 15(1), 14–21.

Joo, Y., Sharifian, M., & Jennings P.D. (2017).*The worldwide transition to renewable energy production and innovation: How financial markets and policies matter*. Paper presented at the Academy of Management, Atlanta, GA.

Jung, C. (2014). *The Archetypes and the Collective Unconscious*. Oxford: Routledge.

Kahan, D., Jenkins-Smith, H., & Braman, D. (2010). Cultural cognition of scientific consensus. *Journal of Risk Research*, 14(2), 1–28.

Karlsson, R. (2013) Ambivalence, irony and democracy in the Anthropocene. *Futures*, 46, 1–9.

Kasser, T. (2002). *The High Price of Materialism*. Cambridge, MA: MIT Press.

Khan, F., Munir, K., & Willmott, H. (2007). A dark side of institutional entrepreneurship: soccer balls, child labour and postcolonial impoverishment. *Organization Studies*, 28(7), 1055–1077.

Kitchin, R., & McArdle, G. (2016). What makes big data, big data? Exploring the ontological characteristics of 26 datasets. *Big Data & Society*, 3(1), 2053951716631130.

Klein, N. (2001). *No Logo*. London: Flamingo.

Kroezen, J. (2014). The renewal of mature industries: An examination of the revival of the Dutch beer brewing industry, (No. EPS-2014–333-S&E). ERIM Ph.D. Series Research in Management. Rotterdam, Netherlands: Erasmus Research Institute of Management. Retrieved from: https://repub.eur.nl/pub/77042.

Kolbert, E. (2014). *The Sixth Extinction: An Unnatural History*. New York, NY: Henry Holt and Company.

Kraatz, M. S., & Block, E. S. (2008). Organizational implications of institutional pluralism. *The SAGE Handbook of Organizational Institutionalism*, 840, 243–275.

Kraatz, M. S., & Moore, J. H. (2002). Executive migration and institutional change. *Academy of Management Journal*, 45(1), 120–143.

Krasner, S. (1988). Sovereignty: An institutional perspective. *Comparative Political Studies*, 21(1), 66–94.

Kuhn, T. (1962). *The Structure of Scientific Revolutions*. Chicago, IL: Chicago University Press.

Kukel, B. (2017). The Capitalocene. *London Review of Books*, 39(5), 22–28.

Kunzig, R. (2015). Germany could be a model for how we'll get power in the future. *National Geographic*, November. Retrieved from: www.national geographic.com/magazine/2015/11/germany-renewable-energy-revolution/

Lassman, P., Velody, I., & Martins, H. (eds.). (2015). *Max Weber's 'Science as a Vocation.'* Oxford: Routledge.

Laumann, E. O., & Knoke, D. (1987). *The Organizational State: Social Choice in National Policy Domains*. Madison, WI: University of Wisconsin Press.

Lawrence, T., & Buchanan, S. (2017). Power, institutions and organizations. In R. Greenwood, C. Oliver, T. Lawrence, & R. Meyer (eds.), *The SAGE Handbook of Organizational Institutionalism*. London: SAGE, pp.417–506.

Lawrence, T., Hardy, C., & Phillips, N. (2002). Institutional effects of interorganizational collaboration: The emergence of proto institutions. *Academy of Management Journal*, 45(1), 281–290.

Lawrence, T., Suddaby, R., & Leca, B. (eds.). (2009). *Institutional Work: Actors and Agency in Institutional Studies of Organizations*. Cambridge: Cambridge University Press.

Lawrence, T., Winn, M., & Jennings, P. D. (2001). The temporal dynamics of institutionalization. *Academy of Management Review*, 26(4), 624–644.

Leca, B., & Naccache, P. (2006). A critical realist approach to institutional entrepreneurship. *Organization*, 13, 627–651.

Lefsrud, L., & Meyer, R. (2012). Science or science fiction? Professionals' discursive construction of climate change. *Organization Studies*, 33(1), 1477–1506.

Leiserowitz, A., Maibach, E., Roser-Renouf, C., Feinberg, G., & Rosenthal, S. (2014). *Americans' Actions to Limit Global Warming, November 2013*. Yale University and George Mason University. New Haven, CT: Yale Project on Climate Change Communication.

LeJeune, K. (2011). Hurricane Rita and the new normal. In M. Hackler (ed.), *Culture After the Hurricanes: Rhetoric and Reinvention on the Gulf Coast*. Jackson, MS: University Press of Mississippi, pp.166–185.

Lewandowsky, S., Oberauer, K., & Gignac, G. (2013). NASA faked the moon landing—therefore climate science is a hoax: An anatomy of the motivated rejection of science. *Psychological Science*, 24(5), 622–633.

Li, C., Singh, A., Klamerth, N., McPhedran, K., Chelme-Ayala, P., Belosevic, M., & Gamal El-Din, M. (2014). *Synthesis of Toxicological Behavior of Oil Sands Process-Affected Water Constituents*. Edmonton, AB: Oil Sands Research Network.

Lounsbury, M., & Hirsch, P. (eds.). (2010*). Markets on Trial: The Economic Sociology of the US Financial Crisis*, Vol. 2. Bingley, UK: Emerald Group Publishing.

Lounsbury, M., Ventresca, M., & Hirsch, P. M. (2003). Social movements, field frames and industry emergence: A cultural–political perspective on US recycling. *Socio-Economic Review*, 1(1), 71–104.

Lyon, T. P., Diermeier, D., & Dowell, G. W. (eds.). (2014). *Corporate Sustainability: Consequences*. Thousand Oaks, CA: SAGE.

Maguire, S., & Hardy, C. (2009). Discourse and deinstitutionalization: The decline of DDT. *Academy of Management Journal*, 52(1), 148–178.

Mann, M. E., Bradley, R. S., & Hughes, M. K. (1999). Northern Hemisphere temperatures during the past millennium: Inferences, uncertainties, and limitations. *Geophysical Research Letters*, 26(6), 759–762.

March, J., & Olsen, J. (1989). *The Organizational Basis of Politics*. New York, NY: Macmillan.

March, J. G., Schulz, M., & Zhou, X. (2000). *The Dynamics of Rules: Change in Written Organizational Codes*. Stanford, CA: Stanford University Press.

Marcus, A., Aragon-Correa, J. A., & Pinkse, J. (2011). Firms, regulatory uncertainty, and the natural environment. *California Management Review*, 54(1), 5–16.

Marquis, C., Glynn, M., & Davis, G. (2007). Community isomorphism and corporate social action. *Academy of Management Review*, 32(3), 925–945.

Marshall, R. S., & Brown, D. (2003). The strategy of sustainability: A systems perspective on environmental initiatives. *California Management Review*, 46(1), 101–126.

Martin, J. (2001). *Organizational Culture: Mapping the Terrain*. Thousand Oaks, CA: SAGE Publications.

McAdam, D., & Scott, W. R. (2005). Organizations and movements. In D. McAdam & W.R. Scott (eds.), *Social movements and Organization Theory*. New York, NY: Cambridge University Press, pp.4–40.

McCright, A., Dentzman,K., Charters, M., & Dietz, T. (2013). The influence of political ideology on trust in science. *Environmental Research Letters*, 8, 1–9.

McCright, A., & Dunlap, R. (2011). The politicization of climate change and polarization in the American public's views of global warming, 2001–2010. *The Sociological Quarterly*, 52, 155–194.

Meadows, D. (2008). *Thinking in Systems: A Primer*. White River Junction, VT: Chelsea Green Publishing.

Meyer, J. W. (2010). World society, institutional theories, and the actor. *Annual Review of Sociology*, 36, 1–20.

Meyer, J. W., Boli, J., Thomas, G., & Ramirez, F. (1997). World society and the nation-state. *American Journal of Sociology*, 103(1), 144–181.

Meyer, J. W., & Rowan, B. (1977). Institutionalized organizations: Formal structure as myth and ceremony. *American Journal of Sociology*, 83(2), 340–363.

Meyer, J. W., & Scott, W. R. (1991). *Organizational Environments: Ritual and Rationality*. Thousand Oaks, CA: SAGE Publications.

Misutka, P., Coleman, C., Jennings, P. D., & Hoffman, A. (2013). Processes for retrenching logics: The Alberta oil sands case, 2008–2011. In M. Lounsbury & E. Boxenbaum (eds.), *Research in the Sociology of Organizations: Institutional Logics in Action*. Bingley, UK: Emerald Group Publishing, pp.131–163.

Mirzoeff, N. (2014). Visualizing the Anthropocene. *Public Culture*, 26(2), 213–232.

Molotch, H. (1970). Oil in Santa Barbara and power in America. *Sociological Inquiry*, 40, 131–144.

Monastersky, R. (2015). The human age. *Nature*, 519, 144–147.

Morris, M., & Patton, P. (eds.). (1979). *Michel Foucault Power, Truth, Strategy*. Sydney: Feral Publications.

Munir, K. (2015). A loss of power in institutional theory. *Journal of Management Inquiry*, 24(1), 90–92.

North, D. C. (1991). *Institutions, Ideology, and Economic Performance*. Cato J., 11, 477.

Oliver, C. (1991). Strategic responses to institutional processes. *Academy of Management Review*, 16, 145–179.

Oreskes, N., & Conway, E. (2010). *Merchants of Doubt: How a Handful of Scientists Obscured the Truth on Issues from Tobacco Smoke to Global Warming*. New York, NY: Bloomsbury Press.

Pache, A., & Santos, F. (2010). When worlds collide: The internal dynamics of organizational responses to conflicting institutional demands. *Academy of Management Review*, 35(3), 455–476.

Palsson, G., et al. (2013). Reconceptualizing the 'Anthropos' in the Anthropocene: Integrating the social sciences and humanities in global environmental change research. *Environmental Science & Policy*, 28, 3–13.

Pedriana, N., & Stryker, R. (2004). The strength of a weak agency: Enforcement of Title VII of the 1964 Civil Rights Act and the expansion of state capacity, 1965–1971. *American Journal of Sociology*, 110(3), 709–760.

Peng, M. W., & Heath, P. S. (1996). The growth of the firm in planned economies in transition: Institutions, organizations, and strategic choice. *Academy of Management Review*, 21(2), 492–528.

Perrow, C. (1999). *Normal Accidents: Living with High Risk Technologies.* Princeton, NJ: Princeton University Press.

Perrow, C. (2007). *The Next Catastrophe: Reducing Our Vulnerabilities to Natural, Industrial, and Terrorist Disasters.* Princeton, NJ: Princeton University Press.

Piketty, T. (2014). *Capital in the Twenty-First Century.* Cambridge, MA: Harvard University Press.

Polhill, J., Filatova, T., Schlüter, M., & Voinov, A. (2016). Modelling systemic change in coupled socio-environmental systems. *Environmental Modelling & Software*, 75, 318–332.

Pope Francis (2015). *Encyclical Letter Laudato Si': On Care for Our Common Home,* Vatican City. Retrieved from: http://w2.vatican.va/content/fran cesco/en/encyclicals/documents/papa-francesco_20150524_enciclica-lau dato-si.html

Popper, K. (1956). Three views concerning human knowledge. *Contemporary British Philosophy*, 387, 357–388.

Powell, W. (1987). Hybrid organizational arrangements: new form or transitional development? *California Management Review*, 30(1), 67–87.

Powell, W., & DiMaggio, P. (eds.). (1991). *The New Institutionalism in Organizational Analysis.* Chicago, IL: University of Chicago Press.

Powell, W., White, D., Koput, K., & Owen-Smith, J. (2005). Network dynamics and field evolution: The growth of interorganizational collaboration in the life sciences. *American Journal of Sociology*, 110(4), 1132–1205.

Rao, H., Monin, P., & Durand, R. (2003). Institutional change in Toque Ville, Nouvelle cuisines as an identity movement in French gastronomy. *American Journal of Sociology*, 108(4), 795–843.

Raskin, P. (2014) *A Great Transition? Where We Stand.* Cambridge, MA: Great Transition Initiative.

Rayner, S. (1992). Cultural theory and risk analysis. In S. Krimsky & D. Golding (eds.), *Sociological Theories of Risk.* Westport, CT: Praeger, pp.83–115.

Reinecke, J., & Ansari, S. (2017). Time, temporality and process studies. In A. Langley & H. Tsoukas (eds.), *The SAGE Handbook of Process Organization Studies.* Thousand Oaks, CA: Sage Publications, pp.402–416.

Rhodes, D. (2014). *Capacity across Cultures: Global Lessons from Pacific Experiences.* Ballarat, West VIC: Inkshed Press Pty Limited.

Rockström, J., et al. (2009). Planetary boundaries: Exploring the safe operating space for humanity. *Ecology and Society*, 14(2), 32.

Rowan, R. (2014). Notes on politics after the Anthropocene. In E. Johnson & H. Morehouse (eds.), *After the Anthropocene: Politics and Geographic Inquiry for a New Epoch. Progress in Human Geography*, pp. 9–12.

Russo, M. (2003). The emergence of sustainable industries: Building on natural capital. *Strategic Management Journal*, 24, 317–331.

Sachs, J. (2008). *Common Wealth: Economics for a Crowded Planet*. New York, NY: Penguin Books.

Scharpf, F. W. (1997). *Games Real Actors Play: Actor-Centered Institutionalism in Policy Research*. Boulder, CO: Westview Press.

Schein, E. (2010). *Organizational Culture and Leadership*, 2nd edn. Hoboken, NJ: John Wiley & Sons.

Schifeling, T., & Hoffman, A. (2017). Bill McKibben's influence on U.S. climate change discourse: Shifting field-level debates through radical flank effects. *Organization & Environment*. doi.org/10.1177/1086026617744278.

Schofer, E., & Hironaka, A. (2005). The effects of world society on environmental protection outcomes. *Social Forces*, 84(1), 25–47.

Schor, J. (2010). *Plenitude*. New York, NY: Penguin Books.

Schussler, E., Ruling, C., & Wittneben, B. (2014). On melting summits: The limitations of field-configuring events as catalysts of change in transnational climate policy. *Academy of Management Journal*, 57(1), 140–171.

Scott, J. (ed.). (1994) *Power: Critical Concepts*, Vol. 3. Oxford: Routledge.

Scott, W. R. (1995). *Institutions and Organizations*, 1st edn. Thousand Oaks, CA: SAGE Publications.

Scott, W. R., & Davis, G. (2015). *Organizations and Organizing: Rational, Natural and Open Systems Perspectives*. Oxford: Routledge.

Scott, W. R., & Meyer, J. (1992). *Organizational Environments: Ritual and Rationality*. London: SAGE Publications.

Seidl, R., Brand, F. S., Stauffacher, M., Krütli, P., Le, Q. B., Spörri, A., & Scholz, R. W. (2013). Science with society in the anthropocene. *Ambio*, 42(1), 5–12.

Selznick, P. (1949). *TVA and the Grass Roots: A Study in the Sociology of Formal Organization*, Vol. 3. Berkeley, CA: University of California Press.

Selznick, P. (1957). *Leadership in Administration: A Sociological Interpretation*. Berkeley, CA: University of California Press.

Senge, P., & Sterman, J. (1992). Systems thinking and organizational learning: Acting locally and thinking globally in the organization of the future. *European Journal of Operational Research*, 59(1), 137–150.

Seo, M., & Creed, W. (2002). Institutional contradictions, praxis, and institutional change: A dialectical perspective. *Academy of Management Review*, 27, 222–247.

Sharifian, M., Joo Y., & Jennings, P. D. (2015). Competing Logics and Innovation in Nation-States: Policy and Patenting in Renewable Energy, 1980–2012. Paper presented at the Academy of Management, Vancouver, British Columbia, Canada.

Showstack, R. (2014). Climate change is 'a defining issue of our time.' Joint Report States. *Eos, Transactions American Geophysical Union*, 95(10), 87.

Sine, W., & Lee, B. (2009). Tilting at windmills? The environmental movement and the emergence of the US wind energy sector. *Administrative Science Quarterly*, 54(1), 123–155.

Slawinski, N., Pinske, J., Busch, T., & Banerjee, S. B. (2017). The role of short-termism and uncertainty avoidance in corporate inaction on climate change: A multilevel framework. *Business and Society*, 56(2), 253–282.

Smets, M., Morris, T. I. M., & Greenwood, R. (2012). From practice to field: A multilevel model of practice-driven institutional change. *Academy of Management Journal*, 55(4), 877–904.

Soskice, D. W., & Hall, P. A. (2001). *Varieties of Capitalism: The Institutional Foundations of Comparative Advantage*. Oxford: Oxford University Press.

Spillman, L. (2002). Introduction: Culture and cultural sociology. In L. Spillman (ed.), *Cultural Sociology*. Malden, MA: Blackwell Publishers, pp. 1–15.

Steffen, W., Crutzen, P., & McNeil, J. (2007). The Anthropocene: Are humans overwhelming the great forces of nature? *AMBIO*, 36(8), 614–621.

Steffen, W., Persson, Å., Deutsch, L., Zalasiewicz, J., Williams, M., Richardson, K., et al. (2011). The Anthropocene: From global change to planetary stewardship. *AMBIO*, 40(7), 739–761.

Steffen, W., et al. (2015). Planetary boundaries: Guiding human development on a changing planet. *Science*, 347(6223): doi.org/10.1126/science.1259855.

Sterman, J. (2001). System dynamics modeling: Tools for learning in a complex world. *California Management Review*, *43*(4), 8–25.

Stockholm Resilience Center. (2016). *Planetary Boundaries: An Update*. Retrieved from: www.stockholmresilience.org/research/research-news/2015-01-15-planetary-boundaries–an-update.html

Stockholm Resilience Center. (2018). *Welcome to the Anthropocene*. Retrieved from: www.anthropocene.info/

Strang, D., & Meyer, J. W. (1993). Institutional conditions for diffusion. *Theory and Society*, 22(4), 487–511.

Swidler, A. (1986). Culture in action: Symbols and strategies. *American Sociological Review*, 51, 273–286.

Thévenot, L., Moody, M., & Lavaye, C. (2000). Forms of valuing nature: Arguments and modes of justification in French and American environmental disputes. In L. Lamont & L. Thévenot (eds.), *Rethinking Comparative Cultural Sociology: Repertoires of Evaluation in France and the United States*. Cambridge: Cambridge University Press, pp. 229–272.

Thornton, P., Ocasio, W., & Lounsbury, M. (2012). *The Institutional Logics Perspective: A New Approach to Culture, Structure and Process*. Oxford: Oxford University Press.

Tolbert, P. S., & Zucker, L. G. (1983). Institutional sources of change in the formal structure of organizations: The diffusion of civil service reform, 1880–1935. *Administrative Science Quarterly*, 28, 22–39.

Tuchman, B. W. (1979). *A Distant Mirror: The Calamitous 14th Century*. New York, NY: Ballantine Books.

Tuma, N., & Hannan, M. (1984). *Social Dynamics: Methods and Models*. Amherst, MA: University of Amherst.

UNFCCC. (2017). *The Paris Agreement, United Nations Framework on Climate Change*. Retrieved from: http://unfccc.int/paris_agreement/items/9485.php

United Nations. (2017). *Global Issues Overview*. Retrieved from: www.un.org/en/sections/issues-depth/global-issues-overview/

Vargish, T. (1980). Why the person sitting next to you hates limits to growth. *Technological Forecasting and Social Change*, 16, 179–189.

Verstegen, J., Karssenberg, D., van der Hilst, F., & Faaij, A. (2016). Detecting systemic change in a land use system by Bayesian data assimilation. *Environmental Modelling & Software*, 75, 424–438.

Vogel, D. (1996*). Kindred Strangers: The Uneasy Relationship between Politics and Business in America*. Princeton, NJ: Princeton University Press.

Warren, R. (1967). The interorganizational field as a focus for investigation. *Administrative Science Quarterly*, 12, 396–419.

Weber, M. (1949). *The Methodology of the Social Sciences*. Translated and edited by E. A. Shils & H. A. Fitch. Glencoe, IL: Free Press.

Weber, M. (1958). *The Protestant Ethic and the Spirit of Capitalism*. Translated and edited by T. Parsons. New York, NY: Scribner & Sons.

Weber, E. (2006). Experience-based and description-based perceptions of long-term risk: Why global warming does not scare us yet. *Climatic Change*, 77(1–2), 103–120.

Weber, K., Davis, G., & Lounsbury, M. (2009). Policy as myth and ceremony? The global spread of stock exchanges, 1980–2005. *Academy of Management Journal*, 52(6), 1319–1347.

Weber, K., Heinze, K., & DeSoucey, M. (2008). Forage for thought: Mobilizing codes in the movement for grass-fed meat and dairy products. *Administrative Science Quarterly*, 53(3), 529–567.

Weick, K. (1993). The collapse of sensemaking in organizations: The Mann Gulch disaster. *Administrative Science Quarterly*, 38, 628–652.

Westphal, J. D., Gulati, R., & Shortell, S. M. (1997). Customization or conformity? An institutional and network perspective on the content and consequences of TQM adoption. *Administrative Science Quarterly*, 42(2), 366–394.

Whiteman, G., Walker, B., & Perego, P. (2013). Planetary boundaries: Ecological foundations for corporate sustainability. *Journal of Management Studies*, 50(2), 307–336.

Williamson, O. E. (1985). *The Economic Institutions of Capitalism*. New York, NY: Simon and Schuster.

Wooten, M., & Hoffman, A. (2017). Organizational fields: Past, present and future. In R. Greenwood, C. Oliver, T. Lawrence, & R. Meyer (eds.), *The SAGE Handbook of Organizational Institutionalism*, 2nd edn. London: SAGE Publications, pp.55–74.

World Commission on Environment and Development. (1987). *Our Common Future*. Oxford: Oxford University Press.

World Economic Forum. (2017). *The Global Risks Report*. Retrieved from: www.weforum.org/reports/the-global-risks-report-2017

World Wildlife Fund (WWF). (2016). *Living Planet Report 2016. Risk and Resilience in a New Era*. Gland, Switzerland: WWF International.

Wright, C., & Nyberg, D. (2015). *Climate Change, Capitalism and Corporations: Processes of Creative Self-Destruction*. Cambridge: University of Cambridge Press.

Young, S., & Dhanda, K. (2012). *Sustainability: Essentials for Business*. London: SAGE Publications.

Zalasiewicz, J., et al. (2016). Working Group on the Anthropocene, Subcommission on Quaternary Stratigraphy. Retrieved from: http://quaternary.stratigraphy.org/workinggroups/anthropocene/

Zald, M., & Denton, P. (1963). From evangelism to general service: The transformation of the YMCA. *Administrative Science Quarterly*, 8(2), 214–234.

Zandbergen, P. A. (2009). Exposure of US counties to Atlantic tropical storms and hurricanes, 1851–2003. *Natural Hazards*, 48(1), 83–99.

Zucker, L. (1983). Organizations as institutions. In S. Bacharach (ed.), *Research in the Sociology of Organizations*. Greenwich, CT: JAI Press, pp.1–47.

Acknowledgments

We appreciate being invited by Royston Greenwood and Nelson Phillips to write for the Elements series. We wish to acknowledge that our ideas and research have benefited greatly from our interactions and publication with many organizations, thinkers, analysts, social observers, and with each other. Andy would like to thank his colleagues at the Erb Institute for Global Sustainable Enterprise, the Graham Sustainability Institute, the Center for Positive Organizations, the Center for Sustainable Systems, and the Management and Organizations group at the University of Michigan for sharing ideas, offering support, and fostering a community of scholars committed to addressing the serious issues we discuss in this Element. Dev would like to thank the Future Energy Systems Research Initiative (FESRI) at the University of Alberta, the Institute for Resource and Environment (IRE, now IRES) at the University of British Columbia, the Canadian Center for Corporate Social Responsibility (CCCSR), and his colleagues in the Alberta School of Business (ASOB) for their research support and the community's commitment to environmental and social sustainability.

Both Andy and Dev have benefited greatly from periodic, long-term interactions with many members of the Academy of Management (AoM) and its Organizations and the Natural Environment (ONE) division and Organization and Management Theory (OMT) division. We would also like to our many graduate students, post-docs, and colleagues with whom we have worked in various capacities on sustainability issues. Some of our interactions (and citations) have worked their way into this Element. Dev thanks Charlotte Coleman, Youngbin Joo, Lianne Lefsrud, Emese Lindstrom, Patricia Misutka, David Patient, Manely Sharifian, Ke Yuan, Milo Wang, Tyler Wry, Paul Zandbergen, and Eric Zhao. Andy thanks Tima Bansal, Max Bazerman, Stephanie Bertels John Ehrenfeld, Jennifer Howard-Grenville, Susse Georg, Nardia Haigh, Rebecca Henn, Willie Ocasio, Lance Sandelands, Todd Schifeling, Marc Ventresca, Judith Walls, and Melissa Wooten. Last but not least, we both would like to thank our mentors, friends, partners, and families for their support in this endeavor. Little in life can be accomplished without the support of these personal communities that surround us. On a final note, for this Element we happily consider ourselves to be equal co-contributors; hence our authorship is alphabetically ordered.

Cambridge Elements ☰

Organization Theory

Nelson Phillips
Imperial College London

Nelson Phillips is the Abu Dhabi Chamber Professor of Strategy and Innovation at Imperial College London. His research interests include organization theory, technology strategy, innovation, and entrepreneurship, often studied from an institutional theory perspective.

Royston Greenwood
University of Alberta

Royston Greenwood is the Telus Professor of Strategic Management at the University of Alberta, a Visiting Professor at the University of Cambridge, and a Visiting Professor at the University of Edinburgh. His research interests include organizational change and professional misconduct.

Advisory Board

About the Series

Organization theory covers many different approaches to understanding organizations. Its focus is on what constitutes the how and why of organizations and organizing, bringing understanding of organizations in a holistic way. The purpose of *Elements in Organization Theory* is to systematize and contribute to our understanding of organizations.

Cambridge Elements ☰

Organization Theory

Elements in the Series

A full series listing is available at: www.cambridge.org/EORT

Printed in the United States
By Bookmasters